MW01123878

DREAMS

DOORWAY
TO
EMOTIONAL
HEALTH

Lloyd E. Shaw

authorHOUSE™

1663 LIBERTY DRIVE, SUITE 200
BLOOMINGTON, INDIANA 47403
(800) 839-8640
WWW.AUTHORHOUSE.COM

© 2004 Lloyd E. Shaw.
All Rights Reserved.

No part of this book may be reproduced, stored in a retrieval system, or transmitted by any means without the written permission of the author.

First published by AuthorHouse 09/21/04

ISBN: 1-4184-0059-9 (sc)   .

Library of Congress Control Number: 2004093286

Printed in the United States of America
Bloomington, Indiana

This book is printed on acid-free paper.

SYNOPSIS

Many books have been written on dreams, but this one is unique. While other books have explained dream symbols and still other books interpret the message of various dreams, this book provides a personalized walk through counseling sessions, revealing how dreams provide a key to the inner problems of individuals. In the step-by- step dialogue reported between counselor and client, the client's problem is revealed through dream analysis. Once recognized by the client, the solution to the emotional problem is readily available.

ABOUT THE AUTHOR

Dr. Lloyd E. Shaw is a retired psychologist and Presbyterian minister. With earned theological and psychological degrees, he conducted a counseling ministry in conjunction with his Gospel ministry work for forty years. He now writes to share his expertise in dream analysis through reporting the dialogue with specific clients in resolving their problems. He resides with his wife, Mary, in Collinsville, IL..

Other books by Lloyd E. Shaw

Wells of Living Water

Reflections of a Twentieth Century Tom Sawyer

God in the First Person

TABLE OF CONTENTS

ACKNOWLEDGMENTS

The production of a book is not possible without the help of a number of people. I wish to thank Betty Calderwood, Helen Nance, and my wife, Mary, for the proofing and editing of this work. Also, I wish to thank AuthorHouse for copy editing work.

In addition to literary help, I wish to acknowledge Clarence Mills and my daughter, Gail Shaw, for assisting me with my computer. Their expertise resolved problems I had with preparing my manuscript for submission to the publisher.

Finally, I wish to thank all my counseling clients whose return to health has filled my heart with happiness through the years. Their emotional recovery has validated my Divine call to be a healer of souls.

PREFACE

"Daddy, I have pictures in my eyes!" That statement was exclaimed many years ago by my three-year-old son, Mark, as he awakened one morning. This childish utterance is a choice pictorial description of a dream. Many times I have referred to dreams as the "late night movie". This statement by my young son years ago was probably a better description of dreams than mine. Whatever we call them, dreams are common to everyone.

Psychologists tell us everyone dreams approximately every ninety minutes during sleep. How do they know that? This knowledge is derived from the study of Rapid Eye Movement (REM) sleep, pioneered by Eugene Aserinsky and Dr. Nathaniel Klitman at the University of Chicago fifty years ago. The REM phase of sleep, in which the eyeballs may be observed moving as if they were watching a tennis game, is associated with clear visual dream images. Volunteers, who were awakened during this time of rapid-eye -movement sleep, reported about ninety-five percent of the time to being awakened during a dream. But if the dreamer wasn't awakened, the dream was almost certainly lost. Dreams melt away quickly. Approximately ninety-five percent of what we dream is never remembered upon our awakening from sleep.

Some people maintain they never dream or they dream very seldom. The reason for this relates to the depth of their sleep pattern. Of the four levels of sleep, only dreams in the first or second level of sleep will be remembered upon awakening. If an individual is in a very deep level of sleep, the dream will be completely erased before the individual arises to consciousness. Some individuals maintain a big meal or heavy drinking before falling asleep causes them to dream more. In fact, it is not the eating or drinking that causes the dreaming. It is their stomach or bladder that disturbs them in sleep, thus preventing them from deep slumber. Being awakened frequently by physical discomforts causes individuals to interrupt their sleep, thus exposing to consciousness more of their dreams than usual.

Having said all this, an answer still has not been given to the question: What is a dream? In lay terminology, a dream is a symbolic pantomime of subconscious emotional feelings. Feelings and emotions such as love, hate, fear, guilt, jealousy, revenge, etc. do not have any physical form. In order to be expressed, these feelings and emotions must clothe themselves in some known form and/or structure. When the mind wishes to expose one of these emotions for personal consideration, it searches around in the archives of personal human memories for some form that will symbolically express the hidden/invisible emotion. This symbolic form is then projected upon the screen of the mind during sleep, and thus the suppressed emotion is expressed through a short pantomime.

This medium of expression through pictures by the sleeping mind is what causes dreaming to appear to be mysterious. Normally, in our waking phase of life, we do not draw pictures to express ideas or feelings. Instead, we use words to convey ideas and meaning. Since thinking in pictures is an unusual and unfamiliar language, it is difficult for most people to understand their dreams. For the dreamer to understand the meaning of the remembered dream, the forms paraded around on the screen of the mind must be analyzed to understand their symbolic meaning.

Dr. Calvin Hall, Director of Dream Research at Santa Cruz, California, in 1975 wrote an excellent book entitled *The Meaning of Dreams*. In his book, Dr. Hall stated that "dreams are not mysterious, supernatural nor esoteric phenomena. They are not messages from the gods nor are they prophecies of the future. They are pictures of what the mind is thinking. Anyone, who can look at a picture and say what it means, ought to be able to look at one's dream pictures and say what they mean."

The message of many dreams is self-evident. This is because a dream is a letter to oneself, a peephole into the subconscious. From my forty year experience interpreting dreams, I believe all dreams have a personal message for the dreamer. Just as an individual interprets the editorial cartoon displayed in the daily newspaper, likewise a dreamer should be able to interpret the picture language of one's dreams. However, if that message would be too painful for the dreamer to admit consciously, then the subconscious mind will disguise its truth in order to protect the dreamer. In such cases, a counselor can gently help the individual interpret the dream so that self-revelation can be revealed to the dreamer.

My first personal experience with dream analysis came as a pastor in Topeka, Kansas in the mid-sixties. The sudden death of a husband produced a counseling situation with the grieving widow. Out of the analysis of a recurring nightmare experienced by the widow, I became aware of the value of dream analysis to emotional health.

The following pages contain documentation of dreams, the interpretation of which has aided me in helping patients restore emotional health. The names of actual individuals have been changed to honor confidentiality. I trust that this documentation of dream analysis, as it relates to ten different areas of emotional concern, will help you understand yourself. The admonition of the philosopher, Socrates, in fifth century B.C., is still true if we are to find emotional health. To his disciples, he stressed the point, "Know thyself". This knowledge of self will never be complete until we understand our dreams. For dreams reveal what we are thinking and feeling within our subconscious mind. True peace of mind involves resolving the internal conflicts disturbing us in sleep. In support of this conclusion, this book has been written, *Dreams: Doorway to Emotional Health.*

Chapter One

-DREAMS-
OVERCOMING GRIEF

-- -- - - - --- - - -

*Dream analysis is a necessary component to grief therapy.
This is true because in the grieving process, the conscious
mind frequently is unwilling to accept reality. Denial persists
because the grieving individual does not want to admit the
loved one is really dead. As long as this denial continues in the
subconscious mind, normal recovery cannot be experienced.
Dream analysis can gauge the extent of emotional acceptance.
When full acceptance of reality has occurred, the dreams of the
grieving person will reveal that fact.*

"Caskets in every room?" I asked.

"Yes," she replied. "In the kitchen, the living room, bedroom,
even in the bathroom! Everywhere there were caskets." The
client, describing her dream, was seated across the desk from
me in my office. Betty was a woman approximately forty-
five years of age. I had conducted her husband's funeral three
months earlier. Although his sudden death from a heart attack
had been a terrible shock, Betty had survived the wake and the
funeral as a normal grieving widow. She appeared at the time
to accept her husband's death with stoic resolve and religious
acceptance.

Now, three months later, she had come to my office in emotional exhaustion. The cause of her turmoil was a recurring dream that had brought her to the edge of a nervous breakdown. Betty said she had not slept for three days and nights. Her face substantiated that fact. This terrifying dream kept repeating itself each time she fell asleep. It was always the same dream with the same dreadful stage props.

She dreamt she was in her home and there were open caskets in every room. When she looked into the caskets, they were all empty. Disregarding the fact that they were empty, the dream was so terrifying, she would wake up screaming, in a hot sweat. The fear of experiencing it again forced her to stay awake but the loss of sleep had brought her to the brink of nervous collapse. I realized if I was to help this woman, I had to interpret her dream and resolve the fear that was disrupting her sleep pattern.

I began by explaining to her that dreams are symbolic expressions of emotional struggles taking place deep in one's subconscious mind. During sleep, these churning feelings come up out of the depths of the subconscious and express themselves in pantomimes on the screen of the mind. Because these feelings have no visual structure in and of themselves, the mind chooses symbolic forms which can be displayed in short pictorial dramas performed on the mental stage. Having explained how a dream is orchestrated, I then began my interpretation by asking Betty a leading question, "What does a casket represent?" She pleaded ignorance to my inquiry but I knew she was hedging the question.

"Oh, Betty, you know what a casket represents," I said with a bantering reply.

She felt the jab of my remark and responded sarcastically: "I suppose you want me to say death?"

"Exactly," I retorted. "A casket represents death. Now we can start to unravel the symbolism of your dream by agreeing that the caskets in your dream represent death." With this insight, the first layer of her terrifying nightmare had been laid open to understanding.

I then proceeded to the next phase. "You told me, Betty, that these caskets were in every room of your house."

"Yes," she replied.

"That would mean, would it not," I continued, "that according to the dream, some-thing symbolizing death is in every room of your house?"

"I guess that is what it is saying," she commented. "But that doesn't make any sense."

Having led her far in her thinking regarding the meaning of the dream, I moved on to another insight in interpreting her nightmare.

"Did you not tell me you looked into those caskets and they were all empty?" I asked.

"Yes," she responded. "They were all empty, but the fact that they were there terrified me and I would wake up screaming."

I settled back a little in my chair and gave a nonchalant shrug so as to relax her before continuing the probing. I pursued our mental quest by stating, "Let's sum up what we have deduced regarding your dream thus far. In the dream, there are caskets in every room in your house. According to symbolic language, caskets represent death. Therefore we must assume the dream is announcing there is something representing death all through your house. Yet, you have reported when you checked those caskets, all were empty." I then asserted: "The message the dream is seeking to announce is there are symbols of death, yet not literal death, in every room in your house. Would you agree with that analysis of the dream, Betty?"

"That sounds right," she replied. But she could not think of anything that would fit such a description.

A novice in dream analysis at that time, I felt I had painted myself into a corner. I believed I was right in my analysis of the dream, but I, too, was stumped regarding the message contained in the symbols. As I sat in silent contemplation regarding this impasse, I prayed desperately to my Lord for Divine wisdom. After a very long minute of silence, the Lord answered my prayer by granting insight to me.

Leaning forward against the desk, I looked directly at the exhausted woman before me and inquired: "Betty, what did you do with Robert's eyeglasses, his Masonic ring, his billfold, his tie clasp?"

The question shook her entire frame. She gasped for air and threw her hand over her mouth. Seeing her shocked reaction, I asked: "What's wrong, Betty?"

Lowering her hand, she spoke in a hushed whisper. "I put them all away in drawers throughout the house, and I have never gotten them out."

The mystery of the dream's message had been resolved. The reason for the terrifying nightmare had been exposed. Based on this revelation of what she had done, I advised Betty: "You go home. Take Robert's personal items and hold them in your hands. Then say to yourself, 'Robert is dead!' I will guarantee, if you do that, you will never have that dream again." Betty went and did as I said. She never had the dream again.

What was going on here? The subconscious mind was struggling with accepting the reality of Robert's death. Although he had died three months earlier, Betty's subconscious mind had not accepted that fact. The clash between reality and her subconscious wish to have him alive created a conflict in her head. Her conscious mind knew her husband was dead, but she had not accepted that truth in her subconscious mind. This mental division between reality and fantasy created conflict in her mind resulting in great internal stress. When sleep relaxed her guard over the subconscious, the struggle came to the surface in the pantomime featuring the caskets in her house.

Once the dream was interpreted, Betty had to acknowledge in her inner being the reality of her husband's death through the handling of his personal effects. This act cleansed the fantasy from her subconscious and forced her to accept reality.

Betty came in for counseling only a few times after this climactic session involving the interpretation of her dream. That interpretation had enabled her to find mental peace through understanding that she had been avoiding reality in her subconscious mind.

****

Betty's situation was not unique. In the years which followed this innovative counseling experience, I have used dream analysis on many occasions to help grieving mates work through the process of bringing reality to their subconscious mind. Especially with younger widows, the acceptance of reality in the subconscious is frequently denied. Even though they consciously know their loved one is dead and they can take you to the grave in the cemetery, this truth is not automatically accepted by their subconscious. When the truth is not accepted by one's subconscious, a prolonged period of counseling is necessary to break through to the inner being and bring reconciliation to the two divisions of the mind.

The method used to find the subconscious truth is to walk the grieving person through the entire episode of loss, starting with the first awareness of the loved one's final illness. Discussion regarding final conversations, and the feelings that erupted when the doctor pronounced the loved one dead, have to be openly shared and discussed. Recalling each painful memory of those final days and hours opens the floodgate of grief and produces waves of tears. Individuals normally have some resistance to talking about these painful memories. Many simply refuse to discuss them, and go into self-imposed mental hibernation. This course of action only prolongs the duration of the grieving period.

To help individuals agree to a series of grief counseling sessions, they are assured the process is necessary in order that they might acquire normal life again. To support my assertion of this needful process, I remind them of the statement of Scripture: "Blessed are those who mourn, for they shall be comforted." (Matt. 5:4)

Jesus, I believe, is teaching us in the Sermon on the Mount that grieving is necessary for the restoration of emotional health. "Unless we grieve," Jesus appears to be saying, "we cannot be relieved of our sorrow which is necessary to acquire the joy of living again." Avoiding talking about that which is painful only prolongs the grieving period.

The need for grief counseling is shown by an illustration taken from everyday life. Discussion of last events and last conversations is comparable to the lancing of a boil. Until the boil is lanced, releasing the pus trapped beneath it, healing cannot begin to take place. Figuratively speaking, the scalpel used for lancing the emotional boil of the grieving mind is directed conversation by a professional counselor.

During the process of grief therapy, an examination of the grieving person's dreams will reveal the progress of subconscious acceptance of reality. The counselor can assure the client of this progress as progressive dreams are analyzed from week to week. Being assured progress is taking place encourages the patient to continue the process required for healing.

An illustration of evaluating the grieving process over time is recalled in the case of a lawyer's wife. Jane's husband died after a prolonged illness. Ten months after his death, Jane came for counseling regarding a nervous disorder. Anxiety and depression were battering her about. She was having great difficulty coping with daily living. After a detailed evaluation of her emotional state, I concluded her problem was her subconscious denial of the loss of her husband. When I inquired if she dreamt about her husband, she informed me that she had many dreams about him.

"Always," she said, "they are very similar." The normal progression of the dream was she would come home from work and walk into the house. Once she had removed her coat and laid her briefcase aside, she walked down the hallway to the doorway of the bedroom. Charles would be in his normal position, sitting up in bed working on some papers. She would speak his name and he would smile at her. Then she would wake up.

Beginning the process of grief therapy, we talked about the details of her husband's long struggle with cancer, and eventual death. She agonized over these memories and expressed various feelings that had overshadowed her during his invalid months. The fact that the recalling of these memories resulted in extensive tears revealed to me she had not yet moved beyond her grieving stage. Through weekly counseling sessions, I applied the healing balm of conversation to her painful mind. Slowly but steadily, the reality of her loss of Charles infiltrated her subconscious mental file. It was a slow process, but the diminishing of tears and emotions from week to week revealed the process was effective. Each week I would check with her regarding what further dreams she had experienced that past week. For a number of weeks, the dreams were always the same. After a few months of counseling, Jane came in for her appointment and said, "I had a different dream."

"Tell me about it," I requested.

"In this dream," she said, "it started out the same. I was coming home from work. I entered the house and walked back to the bedroom just as before. Charles was sitting up in bed working on some legal papers as usual. I spoke his name but he didn't look up. Immediately, in the dream I realized he was dead."

Her dream revealed her subconscious mind had finally accepted the reality of her husband's death. She then found her anxiety and depression were gone. She was normal again. Once again, I learned from a practical situation that dreams, when examined over a period of time, can become the doorway to emotional health.

****

In addition to avoiding reality, many emotions surround the loss of a loved one. A common emotion is fear, fear of losing another person dear to one's heart. Because such a fear is too terrifying to face, it is frequently disguised in the form of a dream. An illustration of such unconscious fear, expressed in a disguised form, occurred in the life of a widow who was left with an only child, twelve years of age. In this case, the dream repeated itself nightly until the grieving mother, Dorothy, was emotionally exhausted.

In a counseling session, Dorothy related the details of her terrifying dream.

In the dream, she commented, "I'm sitting on my porch watching my son ride his bike down the street past our home. At the corner, a speeding car came from across street and hit my son. Immediately, an ambulance crew drove up, lifted my son from the pavement, and raced away with siren blowing." In the dream, she knew her son was killed in the accident and she awoke screaming.

Documenting the various symbols her mind used in this dream, Dorothy noted the symbols involved: her son riding his bicycle, the speeding car, the accident, and the ambulance. After explaining the meaning of each symbol, Dorothy could see the dream was expressing her inner fear regarding the loss of her son. Besides interpreting the dream, I explained why this fear was paralyzing her mind.

Her husband died suddenly at forty-five years of age. She had been totally dependent on him. He had been taken from her, and now all she had left emotionally was her son. The dream was her inner fear the son would likewise be taken from her by death.

Once the dream was explained to her, Dorothy understood its meaning. In subsequent counseling sessions, she learned to cope with the fear of additional loss. The light of understanding caused the dream to cease. Emotional health began to return after the analyzing of her terrifying dream.

****

Another aspect of dealing with grief involves a common concern of grieving people. This concern involves apprehension regarding the spiritual well-being of the departed loved one. Three questions frequently bombard the consciousness of the sorrowing family members: Where are they (the departed one)? How are they? Will we see them again?

At the funeral service, the presiding minister speaks comforting, encouraging words regarding these questions. Yet, regardless of the assurances provided by the officiating minister, it seems a dream can be the most consoling element to the grief-stricken mind of loved ones.

When clients relate a dream regarding the blessed surroundings of their departed loved one, I will concur with the mental picture message portraying a blessed life now enjoyed by the deceased. To do otherwise at this point could be a detriment to the recovery process of the grieving person.

An example of this reassurance transpired in the life of Rhonda, a client. Rhonda, nineteen, experienced the loss of a brother, Larry, at age seventeen. This loss affected her emotional health, filling her with depression and grief. During the course of counseling, she reported the following dream. She was visiting a cemetery and stood beside her brother's grave. She related seeing two angels descending from the clouds. They called out the name of her brother, who in ghost-like form, came out of the grave, and ascended with them through a bright opening in the sky. Once he disappeared from view, she awoke.

That dream lifted the mantle of depression from Rhonda. To her, the message of the dream was self-evident. She interpreted it as meaning all was well with her brother, who was now in heaven. With this assurance filling her mind, she was able to overcome her grief and live life to its fullest. Years later, when I visited with her, she related how the memory of that dream was still a foundation block to her assurance of a life after death. In her case, dreams -*"God's Second Language"*- spoke clearly and distinctly.

****

Sometimes the dream of reassurance is not provided to the grieving family member, but it comes to the dying person. Elmer was such an individual. He was not living life as a Christian. Although baptized and reared as a Christian, as an adult he drifted away from his childhood faith. He eventually became a cantankerous old man.

As his pastor during his sunset years, I faithfully visited him in spite of the fact he maliciously ridiculed the church and me. In my defense, I jokingly sparred with him and kept telling him God loved him. My ministry continued in his behalf while he grew more infirm.

During the last week of his life, when Elmer knew he was dying, I went to his hospital room with some trepidation. Expecting him to cast aspersions on my faith and belief, I walked into his room and asked the usual question, "How are you today, Elmer?" His reply amazed me.

"Fine," he responded. "I am now at peace."

"How did that come about?" I inquired.

"I had a dream," he answered. "Two angels came and visited me. They assured me all was going to be well. They said they would soon be returning to get me and take me to heaven with them. Since that dream," Elmer said, "I have been at peace and I'm ready to go."

Two days later, Elmer died a peaceful death. During the funeral eulogy, I recounted to the gathered mourners his experience with seeing the angels. Sharing his dream experience comforted greatly his widow and all those in attendance.

****

In addition to helping grieving people accept subconsciously the reality of their loss and the fear of future loss, dreams can also enable recovering individuals to start a new life. When a widow or widower begins a new emotional relationship with a friend, guilt feelings arise. Even though legally, they are free to love again, many times they have feelings of being unfaithful to the deceased mate. Grief counseling, using the techniques of dream analysis, can help resolve feelings of false guilt.

Vivian experienced guilt feelings a couple of years after her husband's death, when she first began to date James. We discussed her feelings in a counseling session and I assured her it was false guilt as opposed to real guilt. Logic dictated she should not feel guilty about starting a new life. She had been a faithful wife for forty years. Her husband had been dead for more than two years. Furthermore, she agreed that her departed husband would not want her to be alone. Regardless of her logical decision to begin dating again, Vivian still experienced an internal struggle in her heart. She realized that until this struggle was resolved, she could not move on with her life. What she really needed was approval from her departed husband to proceed with building a new life.

The real freedom from guilt feelings came through a dream. In her dream, her deceased husband appeared and confronted her with a question regarding her new emotional alliance.

"Is James paying your bills?" he asked.

"No," she replied, "I am paying my own way."

Commenting on what had transpired in the dream, I asked: "Was your husband angry with you, regarding James?"

"No," she said. "He just asked if James was paying my bills."

"Then he was admitting the reality of James in your life," I contended.

"Yes, he called James by name but it was without malice," she replied.

That point was significant to her understanding of her problem of guilt. If her deceased husband was not angry regarding her new relationship, then why should she feel guilty? After discussing this point for a few moments, she raised another question.

"But why did I make that reply? I am paying my own bills."

"Perhaps you were providing an excuse for yourself that you were not being unfaithful to the memory of your late husband," I suggested. Although Vivian did not fully understand why her mind had to disguise its message, she understood enough of the dream's message to be greatly relieved. From the dream, she interpreted that her late husband was not angry with her and that he recognized the companionship that James provided. This insight furnished comfortable relief regarding her dating.

What was going on here? This dream portrayed Vivian's logical thinking coming to her from her subconscious mind. Seeing her logic in the form of a pantomime was more impressive than just mere words spoken by a counselor. She believed her deceased husband would approve of her dating again. Yet it was not until this approval was revealed in her dream that she really accepted it. Thus, the dream aided greatly in relieving her guilt feelings regarding her new emotional liaison with a friend.

In the documented cases described above, you can understand the significance dream analysis plays in helping with grief therapy. The problem of overcoming grief involves both the acceptance of the loss of the loved one by the conscious mind, as well as by the subconscious. If the subconscious mind does not accept the loss, the grieving process is not completed. Dreams and dream interpretation can greatly help grieving people move to emotional health. To avoid the use of this tool in counseling will slow the recovery of the patient. Gayle Delaney, a dream psychologist, has spoken of the interaction of dream interpretation and therapy in these words: "Doing therapy without dream interpretation is like doing orthopedics without X-rays." That is my belief also. Therefore, for this reason, dream analysis is part of my work with grieving people.

Chapter Two

-DREAMS-
DIAGNOSING MARITAL
PROBLEMS

Divorce is a prevailing social calamity. Approximately fifty percent of all marriages end in divorce. The reasons for dissolving the marital vows fall into many categories. Chief among them are financial disagreements, unfaithfulness to one another, selfishness, non-sharing of household responsibilities, conflicting lifestyles, etc.

When the cause for marital conflict is known, the justification for divorce is easier to establish. However, in many instances, the cause is elusive. In these situations, the partners cannot precisely identify why they have fallen out of love. They just know they no longer want to be married to the mate. When this happens, it behooves the counselor to seek the cause beneath the level of consciousness for the emotional separation. In my counseling ministry, a number of marriages have been saved through the revealing medium of dream analysis. In cases where the marriage has not been saved, the counseling client has gained constructive insight into the inner self, thus preparing for moving ahead.

Bob and Elaine sought marital counseling due to feelings of emptiness in their marriage. In their mid-thirties, they had been married for seventeen years. I met with them individually and listened to their viewpoints of where they were in their relationship. Both of them assured me they loved each other. Yet both admitted there was no spark of romance in their marriage. Neither Bob nor Elaine could pinpoint exactly the problem, but both felt their marriage slipping away. Both stated lovemaking was almost nonexistent between them. He asserted his sex drive was as strong as ever but Elaine, he said, was not responsive to his advances and frequently rejected his amorous overtures. As a result, he felt distant from her and felt like giving up the struggle to continue the marriage.

Elaine, on the other hand, commented Bob was a good provider. He had been faithful through the years and related well with their teenage daughter. Regarding her emotional feelings for Bob, she admitted that she felt no passion for him. As a result, Elaine conceded that she frequently rejected his sexual initiatives, thus causing hurt feelings on his part.

In a joint session, we discussed their feelings of apathy toward each other. I suggested that they consider a weekend retreat to some nearby vacation spot. Their goal would be to discuss their feelings for each other during a leisurely dinner and then retire to their room where they were to experience the sense of touch to each other's nude body. Only after passion had been sensually aroused were they to engage in lovemaking.

The planned weekend did not produce the desired results. Physical contact through touching did not produce a feeling of emotional closeness between them. They returned from their weekend retreat more frustrated than before. After another round of counseling sessions involving an individual session with each person followed by a joint session, we still were not able to diagnose why they had fallen out of love. Since a conscious discussion of their thoughts and feelings was not revealing the problem between them, I suggest we try to uncover the source of emotional blockage by looking at what was within their subconscious minds. In order to do this, it was suggested that each jot down the details of dreams and be prepared to share them with me at the next interview.

When Elaine came in for her next session, she related a dream exposing the basis of the marital problem. She dreamt they were both in the army in Germany. In her dream, she was manning a machine gun positioned in the center of a road. As she sat behind her gun, she saw her husband running down the road toward her. Seeing him, she said, she opened fire and kept hitting him with bullets until he fell dead directly in front of her. Once he had fallen, she awakened.

"What could be the significance of that dream?" she asked. "I was not in the military service and I have never fired a gun in my life."

"Dreams," I informed her, "are not based on truth. They are symbolic pictures revealing internal feelings. Let us analyze this dream because I believe it has much to tell us. To begin our analysis, why would the location of the dream be in Germany?" I asked.

"I suppose," she answered, "because Bob was stationed there and I went over as a young bride to be with him."

"According to the dream," I said, "something happened while you were in Germany that made you really angry at him. So angry, in fact, that your subconscious mind is still retaining those angry feelings as symbolized in the mental picture of you firing a machine gun at Bob until he falls dead. Do you understand that symbolic portrayal of anger?"

"Yes, it makes sense, I guess," she replied.

I continued probing by asking a direct question. "What happened while you two were living in Germany that caused you to have great anger against Bob?"

The question shook her composure. I could see a change come over her face as she recalled her years in Europe. With tears in her eyes, she finally answered: "When we first were together in Germany as bride and groom, we had considerable adjusting to do. Bob became upset with my independent spirit and slapped me around a number of times that first year. In the years since we have come home, he has not done that, because I learned as a young bride not to challenge his authority."

"I assume, then, you have not fought much in your marriage?" I asked her.

"No," she replied. "Even though I frequently become angry at him, I just bite my tongue and say nothing."

"But you would like to yell at him, would you not?" I inquired.

"Oh, yes," she sighed. "There have been times I would like to have murdered him," she said with a smirk.

"You have just explained the dream," I informed her. "In the dream, you did murder him as you shot him dead with your machine gun."

The root of the problem of Bob and Elaine's marriage had been revealed through this single dream. Repressed anger had blocked the flow of loving emotions from Elaine toward Bob. Now anger was being expressed daily by her passive/aggressive response to him. Rather than expressing her feelings during conflicts, she would hold her tongue and suppress her feelings in her subconscious mind. Over a period of time, this repressed anger built to the extent that it turned off her emotional switch of romantic love.

Bob, on the other hand, was interpreting her rejection of him as a lack of love. Feeling rejected, he responded with less enthusiasm and concern for her personal needs. Unbeknownst to each of them, they were strangling the love that had originally drawn them together.

With this insight regarding the nature of their problem, I began to work with them in resolving their anger. In dealing with Elaine through discussing her feelings, I sought to drain off the anger built up over the years. With Bob, I attempted to help him understand that Elaine's rejection of his sexual advances was not the result of a lack of love, but rather due to repressed anger blocking her normal flow of sexual emotions.

His contribution to her recovery was to confess to her his dominating attitude, and to allow her to express what she really felt without taking it as personal rejection.

My goal was to help them relate to each other by expressing their true feelings at all times. In effect, they had to learn to *fight constructively rather than destructively.* A few months of counseling accomplished this change in their one-on-one encounters. As this change took place, the joy and happiness of their marriage returned.

****

Larry and Barbara had been married eight years. They had a lovely home in the suburbs and were the parents of a girl and a boy. Their lifestyle fit the profile of a successful couple who had obtained the American dream. To observe them interacting in a group setting, you would surmise they were a well-adjusted couple living in a manicured suburb. Behind the facade, however, was a lot of loneliness and frustration, especially on Barbara's part.

Barbara called me one day for an appointment. I detected anxiety in her voice and wondered what could be troubling her. Prior to her call, I had not observed a problem in her life. When we met, she related that she was somewhat depressed and nervous. Life, she commented, was not filled with happiness for her. She hated getting up in the morning and had to force herself to do the necessary tasks of the day.

As we talked about her daily routine, she expressed some guilt regarding her personal feelings. "Why should I not be happy?" she reasoned. "I have a lovely home, I have two darling children, and we have a comfortable income."

In response to her mental pondering, I replied: "Then what is missing in your life? What do you feel you are not getting from your marriage?" She had no immediate reply. I suspected she was not admitting some of her buried feelings. She spoke at length regarding her childhood, her high school romance with Larry resulting in their marriage, and problems with her asthmatic son requiring occasional emergency trips to the hospital. As I listened to her talk about her life, I deducted she had not known personal security in her life.

Larry was not aware of any real problems in their marriage. He had come in for counseling at the request of his wife, Barbara. Life for him was satisfactory. They did not argue much or fight. He admitted he did not feel close to her but he was satisfied with their relationship because he found fulfillment in his work.

After a few sessions of gathering additional information regarding the background of their interpersonal life, I asked Barbara if she had experienced any interesting dreams recently. She replied that she had one dream she remembered because it was so vivid. I encouraged her to relate it to me.

In the dream, she said, she was at home with a terrible headache. Her head, she felt, was swollen to double its normal size. It throbbed with pain. Standing in the kitchen, leaning against the kitchen table, she saw her husband enter the room at the front door. As he walked across the room toward her, she felt great relief because she anticipated he would come to her, put his hands on her head, reduce the swelling, and stop the pain. To her shock, when he approached her, he pulled out a knife and stabbed her in the stomach. At that point, she woke up.

"What does the dream say to you?" I asked.

"I don't really understand it," she replied, "but I know I felt terrible panic when I awoke."

I assured her there was much insight to gather from this dream and I would try to help her interpret it. "Let us begin with the first symbolism expressed by the dream," I commented. "You said the dream opened with you having a swollen head that was throbbing with pain."

"Yes," she replied. "It felt like it was double the normal size and ready to burst."

Picking up on her statement, I sought to lead her further in her thinking by asking: "What does the head represent?"

"When I think of a person's head," she commented, "I think of the brain, or to say it another way, I think of the consciousness, the personality."

"Correct," I assured her. "Your swollen head in the dream represented your self-awareness, which you said was experiencing terrible pain. Isn't that descriptive of why you have come for counseling?" I commented.

"Yes," she replied. "A lot of the times, I feel like I am going to burst inside. My head is so pressured with feelings, I have difficulty thinking straight."

"And why do you feel this internal pressure in your head?" I inquired of her.

"I feel I am not being accepted as a person," she replied.

"And that hurts you a lot," I commented.

"It certainly does," she asserted.

"We understand now why your head hurt in the dream," I commented. "Now let us move on to the next phase of this dream. Human logic would say that anyone suffering from the feeling of non-acceptance would expect one's mate to be understanding and to be there, helping in whatever way possible." I paused for a moment to let that idea connect with her mind, and then I continued building a logical case by stating: "Your dream acknowledged this truth because you said that in the dream, when your husband walked into the room, you felt a great sigh of relief."

"Yes," she agreed, "in my dream, when I saw him enter the room, I felt hope spring up in me that my pain would soon be removed."

"But what did the dream reveal concerning this hope for relief?" I asked.

"I see what you are driving at," she commented. "My hope was based on the expectation that Larry would come and place his hands tenderly on my head and cause the swelling to go down."

"But it didn't happen, did it?" I queried.

"No," she replied. "When Larry approached me, instead of placing his hands on my head tenderly, he stuck me with a knife."

"What do you see in that symbolism?" I inquired.

"I guess it represents how I feel Larry relates to me," was her answer. "Instead of making me feel loved and accepted, when he approaches me, it is only to have sex with me. But once we begin making love, he quickly climaxes and then rolls over and falls asleep."

"And how do you feel then?" I asked.

With a trembling voice, she replied: "I feel used, so I roll over on my side away from him and cry myself to sleep."

"The dream then," I summed up, "is the story of your emotional life. You are aching for acceptance. You expect your husband to provide this. Instead, when Larry approaches you, rather than giving you emotional strokes, he only uses you for his sexual gratification. Have I evaluated your situation correctly?" I asked.

"Yes," she replied with emphasis, "that is the story of my life."

Counseling individually with Larry, I tried to help him understand how his wife felt regarding their relationship. Yet regardless of how I tried to explain her feelings, Larry refused to acknowledge his failure to supply her emotional needs. To him, she was blowing their marital problem all out of proportion. After additional counseling sessions, Larry refused to come any longer because he would not admit he had a problem relating to his wife.

I continued for some time to counsel Barbara. The goal of counseling was to help Barbara gain self-confidence and overcome her feeling of guilt regarding the problem existing in her marriage. Once she accepted the fact that her desires from the relationship were normal, she gained a feeling of self-worth she had not known before. I reminded her that the conflict within her marriage was probably not going to change, since Larry did not see a problem. Therefore, either she would have to learn to cope with it or she would have to terminate the marriage. Eventually, I told her, she would have to make a decision regarding how she was going to handle her marital problem. Some months later, she informed me she was going to seek a divorce. She asserted that she felt strong enough now to take that action. Having arrived at a decision, she terminated our counseling relationship. The last information I heard was she had obtained a divorce and had moved on with her life.

****

Sometimes in marriage counseling, the primary problem is not found nestled in the relationship between husband and wife, but in the baggage that partners bring to the marriage union. This was the case in the marriage of Mike and Anna. This couple had been married only a year when they approached me regarding counseling. They described a relationship which ran hot and cold. One day, they would be relating with love and affection; the next day, they would be fighting over some trivial matter. They both agreed that their marriage could not continue with these extreme swings of emotion.

Visiting with them individually, I tried to determine the cause of their problem. From these initial interviews, the background details of their relationship emerged. Mike was divorced from a wife who had left him for another man. Anna had slept around a lot and was seeking someone with whom she could establish a permanent relationship. They had met in a bar, and after a short time of dating, had moved together into an apartment. Mike was not interested in marriage at first. Anna, on the other hand, felt she needed the security of a marriage relationship and persuaded Mike to marry her.

Once they were married, Mike continued to remain emotionally aloof. He had experienced painful rejection from his first wife. Now he was fearful of committing himself to anyone. He felt comfortable with Anna, but not ready to open himself up to sharing his deepest feelings with her. Even though, at times, he felt like allowing her into his inner self, Anna's hot and cold reactions to him kept him off balance in regard to overcoming his fear of emotional attachment. His aloofness added to her problem of needing acceptance and love.

Anna did not understand Mike, nor did she understand herself. She readily admitted this, as she remarked: "I don't understand myself. I love Mike, but I still lash out at him a lot. It seems I can always find something he has done wrong to become angry about."

I asked her how she had related to men in the past. She informed me that she was always seeking their approval. Her early adult years, she added, were filled with a number of male friends. One man was an abuser with whom she had lived until he finally threw her out in a fit of rage. Others sexually used her, and then dropped her after a short time. One of the appealing things about Mike was that he knew her past conduct but still accepted her.

"During those years, you must not have had a good opinion of yourself," I remarked.

"No," she admitted. "I did not like who I was, neither did I feel accepted by anyone."

"Did you start out as a child feeling loved and accepted?" I inquired.

"No, even as a child, I did not feel loved. My dad never showed any emotion toward me. He never hugged me or kissed me. Never once do I recall him ever saying he loved me." Then with a sigh, she tried to excuse her father by remarking: "Maybe it was the German culture out of which he came. Grandfather had been the same way, cold, reserved, untouchable. All the family members were that way. There was no hugging or touching at our family reunions."

"It sounds to me," I commented, "like you were starved for affection as a child. Do you suppose that is why you tried to get love as you gave yourself freely to the young men you met once you were away from home?"

She thought on that comment for a long moment before answering. "I never thought of it that way," she replied. "I guess I was desperately seeking acceptance. I certainly did not have any personal self-worth, nor did I believe I was desirable. Mike has tried to tell me I am pretty and have worth, but I can't seem to believe him. After he says those things, I begin to think he is just trying to manipulate me into doing what he wants."

"Why do you suppose you cannot accept Mike's statements at face value?" I asked.

She thought on that question a moment and then replied: "I guess because he is a man. All the men I have known never really accepted me as a person. They were only interested in what I could do for them."

"That statement would include your dad, I suppose," I commented.

"Yes," she retorted. "I worked like a dog for him out in the fields on the farm and never once did he say he appreciated what I had done. To him, I was just free labor."

"How do you and your dad get along now?" I queried. "Do you ever go home to visit him?"

"Oh, yes!" she replied. "I go home on holidays and special occasions, but the conversation never involves feelings or discussion of the pain of non-recognition that I remember feeling as a child."

"Would it be safe to say," I commented, "that reconciliation and closure has never occurred between you and your father?

"You are definitely right about that!" she said with enthusiasm.

In our next session, I began the conversation by asking Anna about her relationship with Mike. Previously, Mike had informed me he never knew how he was going to be received when he came home from work. Some evenings, Anna would be smiling and loving. Other days, she would be hostile and brewing for a fight. He had no idea what would trigger one or the other response. As a result, he would avoid a close encounter that she interpreted as rejection.

I began probing the nature of their relationship with a question directed at Anna. "What is it about Mike that annoys you?" I asked.

She fired back with the answer: "He doesn't pay attention to me. He goes out and cuts the grass or he works on his car. Sometimes he expects me to help him with yard work and jobs around the house."

"But aren't those tasks showing love for you through providing you with a nice comfortable home?" I asked.

"Yes, they are," she admitted, "but there is no verbal or physical expression of love. He could at least say 'thank you' once in a while."

"I detect that you feel anger about his conduct around the house," I commented.

"Most definitely," she replied. "I have never told him how I feel, but I still hold him guilty in my heart."

As I listened to her describe Mike's activity around the house, I recalled almost the same ranting and raving being expressed when she talked about her father. Clearly I felt there was a connection between these two men in her mind. In order to help her recognize this fact, I attempted to lead her in that direction by asking another question.

"Do you see traits of your dad in Mike?" I inquired.

With a little laugh, she replied: "Oh, definitely! Sometimes, I think I have married Dad. They are so alike. Mike takes off his dirty clothes and drops them on the floor just like Dad did, leaving Mother to pick them up. But especially," she continued, "I have never felt Mike was completely open to me. Emotionally, there has always been a barrier between us, just like there was a barrier between Dad and me. Dad did not recognize me as a person, and I sometimes feel Mike doesn't recognize me either."

After helping Anna to see that she had similar feelings of anger and separation regarding both Mike and her father, I then suggested to her that perhaps she was tripping over the concept of manhood in her mind. "Perhaps," I volunteered, "you are ascribing to Mike some of the angry feelings left over from your childhood regarding your dad." To further illustrate my point, I added the following pictorial description of what might be taking place. "This would be like a volcano in your subconscious spewing out anger upon Mike."

That thought shook her composure. In her eyes, I could see her mind struggling with the question: What was the source of her anger against Mike? Was she transferring anger she felt toward her father to her husband? After a moment, my suggested analysis seemed to have been reconciled with her thinking. As logic began to prevail within her mind, she responded to my proposed idea by saying: "If that is true, how can I correct my concept of men?"

At this point in our discussion, I suggested Anna make a trip home and try to have an open discussion with her father about her feelings. "Perhaps," I suggested, "an open conversation with your father would help resolve the tension with Mike." She promised to visit her folks before our next counseling session.

When Anna came in the following week, she was in a very good mood. The weekend visit to her parents had been productive. Her parents had moved from the farm and were living in retirement in a nearby community. During the weekend, she found an opportunity to talk to her dad privately. She reported that she told him how she felt he had never accepted her because he never gave her any praise or recognition. To her surprise, her dad admitted his failure as a father and assured her he really did love and accept her. At the end of the conversation, Anna gave him a hug and he hugged her back. On the way home from her visit, Anna felt like she was on cloud nine.

The next week, when Anna came in for her appointment, she related that things were going along better with Mike. They were relating more lovingly, and their marriage seemed to be on an upward swing. In my mind, I felt sure the improvement in relating to her father had been helpful in her relationship with Mike. During our conversation along those lines, Anna mentioned she had a dream the night before. "Perhaps," she said, "if you heard it, you would better understand my inner mind and be more knowledgeable in helping me overcome my problem."

She dreamt her folks had two houses close to each other. One, an old house, the other one, a new one built on a lovely lake. The dream began with Anna visiting her folks in the new house. When she left that house, she crossed the lake to a small house on the other side where she and Mike lived. There was a big bar in their house and half of the house was underwater. Jealously, she followed Mike around in the house, afraid he was going to desert her for one of the girls gathered around the bar. Leaving the bar, they moved into the part of the house that was underwater. While underwater, she had no trouble breathing, but she had very bad vibes. When they would come up out of the water, the vibes were good. With those contrasting feelings going through her mind, she awakened.

I began analysis of the dream by asking: "Do you see any insights in your dream that reveal truth about yourself?"

"No," she replied. "It seems very confusing. I don't see any meaningful truth regarding myself in the dream."

"Before we discard it as mumbo jumbo," I volunteered, "let us look at some of the symbolism portrayed in the dream. Perhaps it is revealing something about which you are not aware." I continued the analysis by asking: "In the dream, how many houses did your folks have?"

"There were two houses," she replied. "One was an old dark house and the other one was bright and new. Yet, that is not true because my folks only own one house."

"Oh," but I replied, "Disregarding the fact that your folks only have one house, symbolically, I believe, this dream is true."

"How can you say that?" she asked.

"Because," I continued, "I believe you told me your original relationship to your home was one that was cold and unhappy. But this last time, after you went home for a visit, you came away all excited and happy. Symbolically speaking, couldn't that be portrayed as two different houses?"

"Yes, I see what you mean," she said excitedly. "My mental vision of home does involve one place dark and foreboding while my parents' home now is seen as a warm, loving place."

Continuing with my analysis, I commented: "According to the dream, you left your parents' new house and crossed a lake to another house where you and Mike live. In that house, there was a bar with girls standing around. Does that say anything to you?" I asked.

"Oh, I think I understand the symbolism of the bar," she volunteered. "It was in a bar that Mike and I met. But I don't understand why there are girls in my house."

"Let's think about this a moment," I retorted. "Didn't you tell me you didn't understand yourself? I am sure you were referring to the fact you keep changing in your feelings toward Mike. One day, you love him; the next, you are yelling at him."

"Yes, I do that," she replied.

I continued to lead her in her thinking by suggesting: "Then wouldn't it follow that for your mind to express in picture logic the various moods you express, it would have to use multiple girls. Figuratively speaking, therefore, there are different girls in your house, and they are all you."

"Touché!" she cried. "I do manifest different personalities. And I worry about which Anna Mike will like."

"You see, there is a lot of truth in this dream. Let us go on to still another significant insight concerning yourself. Let us look at the matter of your house being half submerged in water. Do you see any relevance to this symbolism?" I asked.

"No," she answered. "Our house is not near any water."

"Don't think of it as water, per se," I commented. "A dream uses picture language to present its message. Since an emotional feeling has no form, water could represent the relationship existing within your home between you and Mike could it not?" I continued by saying: "You told me you didn't understand Mike. This means only part of your relationship with Mike is consciousness while part of it is in the subconscious. Could not your mind be using the symbolism of water to depict your house, representing your emotional relationship with Mike, is half out of water and half underwater? Furthermore," I reasoned, "this explanation seems logical, since in the dream, you specified that you had no trouble breathing under water."

"Your analysis makes sense," she commented. "But why did I have bad vibes while underwater and good vibes when I was above the water?"

"That explanation is simple," I pointed out. "You have told me the thing which bothers you about Mike is you don't understand him. That means underneath the level of your consciousness, you are disturbed by things you don't understand. In areas where you two consciously relate well, you are happy and content."

"My dream had a lot of truth in it, didn't it?" she said. "Now I think I see the basis of my problem. If I understand the dream correctly, my problem with Mike involves something in my subconscious mind."

"Exactly," I assured her. "And I am suggesting the subconscious problem is suppressed anger relating back to your feelings against your father. Those feelings, erupting like a volcano deep within your mind, are spewing out anger upon Mike. As you expand on your reconciliation and closure with your father, thus removing buried anger from the past, you should continue to draw closer to Mike."

Anna accepted that analysis of the dream. In the weeks that followed, she visited her father a number of times and continued to build a wholesome relationship with him. As she did that, her relationship with Mike improved. Week after week in counseling, she became more aware of her inner self. Through deep conversations with Mike, their bond of love strengthened. In a few months, they felt their relationship was strong enough to proceed on its own. At that point, we terminated our counseling relationship.

Chapter Three

-DREAMS-
EXPOSING SEXUAL ABUSE

Sexual abuse results in lifelong emotional problems. To those who remember the personal trauma, psychological help can enable the abused person to overcome emotional damage caused by the abuse. In other cases, however, the victim may not remember the dehumanizing experience. This forgetfulness is a technique of the human mind to protect the victim through submerging the terrifying experience deep in the subconscious mind. Submersion, however, does not remove the problem. Sooner or later, the effects of the sexual abuse will erupt from the mind's depth and cause individuals emotional problems. When these problems manifest themselves in the lives of victims, the obligation of the counselor is to expose and remove these disturbing subconscious feelings. In order to accomplish this task, dream analysis is occasionally the expedient tool bringing about emotional health.

Rose was thirty years old, married, and the mother of two young children. In making her appointment, she had requested marriage counseling. We began our conversation by inquiring about the nature of her marriage. She informed me she and her husband, Bill, had been married eight years. In the early years of their marriage, things had gone well between them. Once their first child, Teddy, was born, their sexual life tapered off because she lost interest. Yet, in spite of fewer occasions of lovemaking, she became pregnant again and had a daughter, Julia. "Since then," she said, "there has been constant conflict in our home." She admitted she felt guilty for considering it but divorce had begun to enter her mind.

We talked further about her tangled web of feelings regarding her life and marriage. I suspected she was carrying a lot of baggage from earlier years. Following a hunch, I asked her to tell me about her childhood and early life.

Rose related that her early years were spent in Florida. Many bad memories were associated with those childhood years. Especially, she remembered being frequently left alone. Her father and mother both worked. Many times, her parents would go to a tavern and leave her home alone. When she was in first and second grade, her parents would feed and dress her in the morning, then leave her to wait alone until it was time for school. After school, she came home to an empty house. On one occasion, in second grade, two black boys groped her with their hands.

When Rose was eight and in third grade, her parents divorced. Rose and her mother moved to the Midwest to be near her grandparents. There she spent most of her time at her grandparents' house, where her grandfather became her chief babysitter while her mother worked in a bar. The grandmother worked the afternoon shift, leaving Rose to sleep at her grandparents' house. Frequently, she would sleep with her grandfather until her grandmother came home from work.

A number of these related experiences raised red flags regarding her psyche's development, but I let them pass without comment at the time. In our next counseling session, I inquired about her early teen years. Rose admitted she became sexually active at thirteen. When her mother learned of her conduct, she started Rose on birth control pills. Not fearing pregnancy,

Rose's high school years were one continuous succession of involvement with boys. In her mind, Rose did not perceive sexual involvement as being used by boys; rather, she thought of it as using them. When Rose was in college, she met Bill. Although she had been sexually active with many young men, Bill appealed to her because he did not make sexual passes at her. He treated her as a lady, making her feel good about herself. After a year of dating, Rose married Bill upon his graduation.

When our conversation returned to how she felt about her husband, Rose expressed considerable anger toward Bill. I questioned her regarding what Bill was doing to incur so much anger. In her comments about him, Rose appeared to be trying to discredit his manhood by accusing him of being a latent homosexual. She wanted him to confess to her that he was a homosexual. Bill's refusal to do so only increased her anger toward him. In her angry state, Rose lashed out at men in general and said they were all rotten and useless. In light of her attitude toward men, I suspected there was some sexual trauma in her background. The logical culprit would be her grandfather.

In one of our counseling sessions, I floated the unmentionable issue. "It appears to me," I stated, "that you may have been sexually abused by your grandfather." Rose flew to her grandfather's defense by asserting, "No way! Grandfather was the only family member who loved me. He would take me out to get ice cream, and we would play games together." On and on she spoke in glowing terms regarding her grandfather. Rose's defense of her granddad reminded me of a scene in Act III of Shakespeare's play, HAMLET. As the Queen observed the denial of a player regarding her plot in the murder of her husband, the Queen was led to say: "Methinks, the lady doth protest too much." Well, I perceived Rose was denying too much her grandfather's guilt.

Although Rose asserted she had no memory of sexual abuse, I was determined to seek the truth on her behalf through an indirect approach. This approach involved encouraging her to record her dreams and share them with me the following week. When Rose returned for her next session, she came prepared to report her nocturnal pantomimes.

She dreamt, she said, she was in the basement of a house. There was a bed there against the wall. Some man was there but he had no face that she recognized. She was terrified he was going to hurt her. The man had a dog that approached her and licked her shoes. While being filled with terror regarding her safety, she awakened.

"It sounds like it was a scary nightmare," I ventured.

"It was," she admitted. "I did not recognize the man, but I was sure he was going to rape me."

"Did your grandfather's house have a basement?" I asked.

"Yes," she replied. "But I do not remember any bad experiences happening there."

"One aspect of the dream appears to be speaking loudly," I commented. "I am referring to the dog licking your shoes. The mind substitutes scenes and faces when the revelation would be too painful for the dreamer to accept. A case in point could be the dog licking your shoes. Do you have any recollection of oral sex being performed on you by your grandfather?"

Rose was shocked speechless by the question so she responded in the negative with a shake of her head. After a pause, she spoke, saying: "Since we talked last week, one memory has come to me and it has always bothered me. I remember once when I was about eight years old, awakening from sleep in my grandfather's bed, and there was blood on my panties. I mentioned it to my mother and she told me to forget it."

"Your mother wasn't concerned about your being with your grandfather?" I asked.

"No, instead she always tried to make me look pretty when I went to his house. She would dress me in my best dresses before she dropped me off there on her way to the tavern."

Rose's past was beginning to come into focus. Still, she defended her grandfather regarding any evil conduct. After further discussion regarding the bloody panties, Rose did promise to speak to her mother and grandmother regarding details of her early years. When she returned for her next therapy session, Rose informed me her mother and grandmother were both adamant against her digging into the past. "Nothing happened," her grandmother emphatically said, "and you should not be afraid to leave your children over here." That statement was in reference to the fact that Rose had refused to let anyone baby sit her children, especially the grandparents. Learning of this restriction regarding child care, I now suspected the age of her daughter was probably the catalyst bringing Rose's submerged trauma to the surface now, indirectly causing her to seek counseling.

The following week, Rose had another dream to share. In this dream, she was shopping at the local mall with an unknown friend. A black man ripped off her earrings. In panic, Rose and her friend quickly exited through the door only to discover they could not re-enter the mall. Realizing this, they ran to her white van. Rose made it safely but her friend did not. She saw her companion being caught, stripped, and wrapped in Saran Wrap. Seeing the terrifying scene unfold, Rose drove away in panic to a McDonald's restaurant, where she ran into the restroom. Even there, she felt someone was coming after her.

"You have had another very illuminating dream," I assured her. "Let us interpret the symbolism which it has portrayed. To begin, let us assume the black man does not refer to a racial person but represents the evil person who has harmed you. The second symbol is more disguised. What do you associate with earrings?" I asked.

She thought a moment and then answered: "I guess I would say my femininity. When I put on earrings, I feel like I am a beautiful woman."

"Good!" I responded. "Let us assume then the dream is saying an evil man has ripped away your femininity, literally your wholesome sexuality." I continued the interpretation of the dream by adding: "If the mall represents the abundant life, then once your femininity was lost as you exited the store, you cannot go back in because you have lost your childhood innocence."

"Yes, I can see that," she replied.

"The next symbolism of the dream is your friend being caught and wrapped in Saran Wrap," I commented. "Could it not be that the other person who was caught and wrapped in Saran Wrap was your alter ego? I perceive you as a split personality. A part of you has gone on with your normal life after having lost your childhood innocence through being abused. This is illustrated by your driving the car away to a McDonald's restaurant, representing the onward progress of your life. The other part of you has been stripped and exposed by your grandfather's abuse, as portrayed by the Saran Wrapped person."

"That all certainly makes sense," Rose responded. "I have felt for a long time that I am a duel personality. Perhaps that explains something else that has been a puzzle in my life that Bill has accused me of doing. When we make love, I enjoy myself but then a half hour later, I lash out at him in anger."

"I think you have diagnosed correctly that pattern in your conduct," I complimented her. "Sex, in your mind, is interrelated with feelings of guilt, shame, and trauma. Even while you enjoy sexual intercourse, those negative feelings are aroused in your mind and you express them later by hating the one who has aroused you sexually."

We talked at length about the interaction between Bill and her. Definitely, Rose's warped concept of love caused by her mother's and grandparents' conduct resulted in marital problems for her. They told Rose they loved her, yet their actions showed her no concern or acceptance. Especially when she had expressed statements about being violated, they criticized her and told her to be quiet. Now, as an adult, when Bill spoke the endearing words, "I love you," Rose's mind did not respond with the right emotions. As her counselor, I spent much time talking about this problem of distorted word association. Only time would tell whether Rose could sort out the correct feelings in her heart to continue the marriage.

The last symbolism in the dream, I explained to her, related to her distorted mental wiring regarding sex. "Remember, you said in the dream that when you arrived at the McDonald's restaurant, you ran into a restroom. There you felt somebody was still going to get you," I commented. "That part of the dream," I pointed out, "most likely refers to the fact that your sexual abuse is always with you and continues to fill you with fear. This fear will be especially evident when you are engaged in sexual activity or toilet activities pertaining to sexual organs. This irrational fear will remain with you until you have overcome it."

We talked at great length about the symbolism of the dream and the feelings associated with each part of her mental pantomime. Rose had now accepted the fact that she had been sexually abused but she was having a lot of trouble feeling anger toward her grandfather for what he had done. Because he had shown concern for her in contrast to the other members of the family, Rose continued to put him on a pedestal. I knew Rose would never totally disown him but I hoped she could develop a love/hate relationship as she became more aware of how he had deformed her psychic life.

More of her submerged past began to burst into her mind as we continued counseling. An incident of past memory was resurrected by a household appliance. Rose imagined she heard a strange noise in her refrigerator. She called a repairman who came and checked her appliance. The repairman informed her there was nothing wrong with her refrigerator. A week later, Rose had a second serviceman come and check the refrigerator with the same conclusion. When Rose told me of her annoyance regarding the refrigerator noise, I commented on her concern.

"Since two repairmen have confirmed there is nothing wrong with your appliance," I suggested, "we need to look at this noise you are hearing from a psychological viewpoint. What do you associate with the sound of a refrigerator?"

A frown came over her face before she replied. "I remember," she commented, "there was a refrigerator against the wall of grandfather's bedroom. When I would lie in his bed, I would hear it running."

"You have solved your refrigerator noise," I assured her. "You probably concentrated on the sound coming from beyond the wall to block out what was being done to you. Now that your blocked-out memories of childhood are coming to the surface, the memory of the refrigerator noise is preceding the recollection of your trauma. This process is normal and necessary for regaining your mental health." Rose's face lit up with insight as she listened to my explanation of the troubling noise annoying her.

.At this stage in counseling, Rose was determined to know the full truth. She decided to confront her grandfather regarding events of the past. Taking Bill with her for moral support, Rose went to her grandfather's house and engaged in a conversation about childhood events. Grandfather violently denied involvement in any sexual abuse, and asserted that if there was any, it was done by her father. At one point in the confrontation, when Bill tried to argue a point, the grandfather threatened to hit him. While this was taking place, the grandmother was screaming that Rose was crazy to imagine such a thing had happened. Seeing the conversation had gotten out of hand, Rose and Bill left. As a result of the confrontation, the grandfather fell off his pedestal in Rose's mind. She was now convinced her grandfather was guilty of sexual abuse.

We talked about this development at our next counseling session. More and more of the submerged memories were coming into focus. Rose was seeking to deal with them in her life. A few weeks later, she related to me another dream. In this dream, Rose dreamt she was walking into her grandparents' house. It was dark. When she stepped through the door, she felt real fear because she knew someone was there. Rose walked into one bedroom and saw a cigarette lighter on a stand. It glowed in the dark. Picking the lighter up, she continued walking through the house. As she walked by another bedroom door, Rose heard her grandfather snoring. She was afraid she would awaken him so she tiptoed past his door while experiencing great fear. Rose got to the front door without awakening her grandfather and went outside. Once outside, she didn't know which way to go. At that point, she awakened.

Hearing the details of this dream, I immediately cried out: "Wonderful! That is the best news I have heard regarding your case."

"How is that?" Rose remarked. "What was so wonderful about that dream?"

"Well, let us look at what the pantomime is saying," I commented. "I believe that when we interpret the message conveyed by the dream, you will agree also that it is wonderful news. First," I began, "you said as you entered your grandparents' house, you had great fear. This is natural because that was the house in which you had experienced unspeakable horrors. Is that not true?"

"Yes," Rose responded, "whenever I drive past that house now, I feel the creeps."

I continued the interpretation by stating: "OK, next you mentioned finding a cigarette lighter that glowed in the dark, I believe?"

"Yes," Rose replied, "it was lying on a stand and it glowed in the dark."

"What does a lighter symbolize to you?" I inquired.

"I guess I associate it with fire," Rose replied.

"Would you add to that association light?" I suggested.

41

"Yes," she agreed. "A lighter provides fire which gives light."

"Could we transpose insight for light?" I suggested.

A light bulb went on in Rose's mind and she exclaimed: "Now I see it! The lighter represents the insight I have gained from counseling. I picked it up and have used it to understand myself."

I continued unraveling of her dream by adding: "Now for the most important piece of the puzzle. You said you tiptoed past your grandfather's bedroom door while he was sleeping. It would seem to me that part of the dream is saying your grandfather is no longer active in your mind. Rather than being there as the unknown person in the basement dream, or as the black figure in the mall dream, now the mysterious person is acknowledged in your dream as your grandfather but not active in your life. Isn't that good news?" I asked.

A smile swept across Rose's face. With excitement, she spoke, saying, "It sounds like we have come a long way in dealing with my problem. Hopefully, I can continue to sort out the ramifications of my emotional trauma."

I commented that the concluding scene of the dream spoke to that very problem. She had reported that after she left the house and went outside, she didn't know where to go. The message of this scene described her present circumstances. Rose now had insight; she had knowledge of her sexual abuse; but she still had a long way to go to be completely free of her disturbing inner feelings.

The crest had been crossed on Rose's road to recovery. We continued to counsel together for a few more months. Eventually, Rose and her family moved from the community, thus breaking our contact. My hope, when I concluded counseling with her, was that Rose would find the abundant, happy life she deserved.

****

The human mind can be compared to a file cabinet. Every experience we have in life is filed away there as a memory. Not only are all the good memories filed there for later recollection, but all the bad experiences are also thrown in there, where they form a mental rubbish heap. Each of us has a rubbish heap in our mind. In most cases, our personal rubbish heap does not contain any toxic memories imposing on our normal daily activities. For the average person, bad memories only cause some disturbing nightmares or abnormal lifelong fears. These negative memories are usually controllable for the average person.

In cases where there has been sexual abuse however, the traumatic memories buried in the victim's mental rubbish heap continue to hold potential danger. Such psychological rubbish can paralyze a person to the point where he or she cannot function. When this happens, counseling is required to disperse the rubbish heap and restore the individual to more normal mental health.

Lois was an example of one whose rubbish heap eventually disrupted her normal daily activity. Lois was a single lady, forty years of age. Her profession involved working as a desk clerk in a city office. In this position, she was constantly encountering the public and filling out forms for them. Lois was aware that she was experiencing temporary memory loss while visiting with people, especially men. Hearing a name or personal information, she would occasionally go blank in her mind and be forced to ask the same question over again. Realizing she had a problem, Lois called for a counseling appointment.

When Lois presented herself across the desk from me, I began our meeting by inquiring regarding the nature of her problem. "What is your problem?" I asked. "How can I help you?"

Lois described her situation in these words: "I am having mental blackouts. When people approach my service counter, I need to ask them certain questions in order to complete their application for city services. Sometimes when they speak, I draw a blank and cannot remember what they have just said, so I have to ask them to repeat themselves. It is very embarrassing. I don't think I am losing my mind but I sometimes wonder."

"I am sure that must make you very nervous," I commented.

"It most certainly does!" she replied. "I am so uptight over the fear that it is going to happen again, I frequently make mistakes."

I asked her how long this problem had been affecting her. Lois informed me it had started only about a month before. I continued our line of thought by inquiring if anything extraordinary had transpired in her life recently. She informed me that everything had been normal. She was living the same lifestyle she had always lived. After discussing at great length her life and general physical health, I could find no evidence regarding the source of her problem. Yet something was causing her extreme anxiety, resulting in temporary blackouts in her memory.

At our next counseling session, I continued my probing of her personal life. "Have you experienced feelings of anxiety in other situations?" I asked.

"Yes," she admitted. "I am finding I am afraid of being around people. Lately, I have been staying in my home most of the time. I have difficulty going out to the shopping mall. More and more, I am limiting my personal activities."

"It sounds like you are becoming afraid of daily life," I commented.

"Yes," she said, "I am becoming paralyzed with fear. I don't know what I fear, but I know I am losing my ability to function."

"What you have described is an irrational fear," I commented. "Yet irrational or not, it has as much power to paralyze your activity as real fear does."

At our next session, in order to unmask her problem, I began quizzing her regarding potential areas of fear in her life. "Do you fear losing your job?" I inquired.

"No," she answered. "My boss says he is well satisfied with my work. I have no worries in the area of employment."

"Do you have conflicts with fellow employees?" I asked.

"No, I like the people I work with," was her reply.

After much further discussion covering many potential problem areas, I was still not able to detect any apparent area of fear or anxiety that was troubling her. I then turned the conversation to an emotional level.

"Now that you have turned forty," I commented, "do you fear getting old, eventually dying?"

"I don't think so," she remarked. "Naturally, I would like to stay young, but I realize that the years roll by and we all eventually grow old. I don't think much about death, but I can't say the concept troubles me."

After all our discussion, we had not exposed anything giving foundation to her extreme anxiety. Being frustrated in my initial search for a cause of her emotional disorder, I directed Lois to monitor her dreams and come prepared the next week to report on her nocturnal fantasies.

When Lois came in for her next appointment, she was prepared to give a report. She began by saying: "My dream did not have any significance. I don't believe it is worth repeating."

"Tell me anyway," I directed. "Let me determine if it has a message or not."

"My dream," she related, "involved my pet hobby. I like to work in my yard. In my dream, I was working in my yard, trimming my rose bushes. My father, who passed away a year ago, was helping with the trimming. We didn't speak, but the two of us were busy pruning and weeding around the yard. After what seemed like a few minutes of this activity, I awakened."

The dream sounded perfectly innocent. Yet in spite of its flawless picture, I knew it could still hide a disturbing message. To help in discovering its subliminal message, I related to Lois a counseling experience that had transpired about a year before.

In that case, I was counseling with a kleptomaniac regarding the motivation as to why she had been arrested for stealing. The patient had informed me she did not know why she had an urge to steal. She didn't need the stolen items; mostly she threw them away after she returned home from shopping. Why then did she steal items? I had wondered.

When no apparent reason was forthcoming to explain her thievery, I related to Lois how I had switched to a different approach in seeking to uncover the truth. "Tell me," I had asked my client, "what was the first thought that went through your mind when the policeman grabbed your arm in the store?" She thought a moment and then, smiling, said: "I remember the thought but it doesn't make any sense."

"Tell me," I had requested.

"Well, I remember," she said, "I thought: Now I will get to see Mother. But what is significant about that?"

"I think you have just explained your hidden motivation," I asserted. "Remember you told me of an experience that happened in your childhood. Your parents were divorced when you were five. You were sent to live with your mother and you were promised that when your mother remarried, she would take you with her. Yet when your mother did remarry, you told me your mother did not come and get you. Instead, you continued to live with your grandmother until you were caught stealing empty pop bottles and selling them back to the grocery-man for the deposit of two cents each. When that happened, your grandmother said: 'Since I can't control you, you will have to go home to Mother.' Getting back to Mother was accomplished through stealing, was it not?"

"Yes," she admitted. "For me, stealing provided me with what I wanted."

"Does that not explain your subconscious motivation for stealing now also?" I asked her.

"Yes," she had replied. "Now I see my inner motivation was to go home to Mother."

That statement explained my client's motivation for stealing. I explained to Lois that my patient had been twenty-three, divorced, and burdened with a lot of problems. She subconsciously wanted to go home to Mother, where she could feel secure, like a child. The way her subconscious mind chose to bring that about was by getting caught stealing, just like when she was a child. Once my client understood the subliminal motivation for her action, she was cured of shoplifting.

Having told this story to Lois, I redirected our attention to continual analysis of her dream. "Your dream," I said, "involved a pleasant picture of working in your yard, but let us looks for a subliminal message. What thought," I asked, "went through your mind as the dream was unfolding in your mind?"

Lois thought on that for a moment and then replied: "As I leaned over, trimming the roses, I felt Dad looking at my legs and hips." Hearing that, the answer to her emotional problem jumped out at me. Quickly, I put the question to Lois: "Did your father ever rape you?" I asked.

Tears came to her eyes and she dropped her head. After a pause, she replied: "Yes, a few times when I was about eleven years of age, before he started to attend AA meetings."

The garbage heap in her mind holding toxic waste had finally erupted into her life. Further counseling revealed the trigger projecting the sexual abuse to the surface was the anniversary of her father's death, plus her interest in a gentleman friend. Due to her blossoming romance, sexual feelings were beginning to be aroused within her. Now memories of Lois's father's action were extracted from the subconscious into her conscious mind. For years, those traumatic memories had laid buried because she did not want to think about them. Yet, when her subconscious mind paraded feelings on the screen of her mind in sleep, those repulsive memories sneaked into her nocturnal pantomimes as a separate thought, rather than a picture. Concentrating our analysis on the thought associated with the dream, the hidden truth producing her anxiety was exposed.

Further counseling enabled Lois to unearth those submerged feelings and eventually restore tranquility to her troubled mind. Once this happened, the incidents of experiencing occasions of blank memory ceased. Lois still carries the scars of sexual abuse, but she is now able to function comfortably while performing daily activities.

Chapter Four

-DREAMS-
SOURCE OF VALIDATION

Social scientists tell us there are four basic needs necessary to maintaining human life. They are food, clothing, shelter and water. In addition to these basic needs, there are additional requirements essential to making life meaningful. One of those is validation. We all are forced by necessity to make daily decisions. Joy comes when another person validates us by assuring us we made the right decision. Without validation, we frequently experience the pangs of uncertainty. Validation gives us self-worth and confidence. In some cases, the needed validation comes through dreams.

It was a heavy burden. The burden bearer, Sarah, was nineteen, single and a college student. She had recently been forced to assume a crushing load. Two months previously, her middle aged mother died suddenly from a malignant brain tumor. Owing to this dreadful event, Sarah was projected into the role of chief cook and homemaker for her father and younger brother. Stoically, Sarah shouldered the responsibility and bent to the task, fulfilling her new role in the home. There was no time for personal grieving. While her father and brother shed tears of sorrow, Sarah threw herself into the daily tasks that fell to her lot.

A few weeks after the family loss, Sarah stopped by my office for a chat. Being a relative of mine, she felt she could talk about an issue troubling her. With some trembling in her voice, Sarah voiced her concern. "It appears," she said, "I am going to have to drop out of college."

Her statement shook me deeply because I knew how devoted she was to obtaining her college degree. "What is the trouble?" I asked her. "Are the classes too hard? Are you finding you are too busy to study?"

"No," Sarah replied with trembling voice, "I enjoy the classes and I know I can make the grades. No, the trouble is...the walls of the lecture room are moving in on me. I feel claustrophobic."

"You feel the walls moving in like they were going to crush you?" I responded.

"Yes," Sarah lamented. "Our classroom is in a basement and there are no windows. It has gotten so bad for me I can't sit in that room."

I was surprised by her revelation. I thought of her dear dead mother and how upset she would have been to hear her daughter's plight. Quickly, I sought to assure Sarah that her problem was psychological and it could be resolved. I suggested she seek counseling immediately. She informed me she would accept counseling but only if I worked with her. I strongly objected to her request because of our family relationship. However, under pressure of her pleading, I agreed.

I felt confident the claustrophobia Sarah was experiencing was caused by emotional pressure. Certainly, the changes occurring in her life throughout the past month were enough pressure to drown anyone. Nevertheless, I also knew that until Sarah herself could recognize the source of her emotional conflict, those walls would not stay in place.

I began helping Sarah cope with her problems by asking about the pressures in her life. "How are things going at home?" I inquired.

"Oh, we are getting by OK," Sarah replied. "I have developed a routine for preparing meals and Dad is helping with the dishes. Since Dad never did grocery shopping, I have assumed that task also. He gives me money and I go to the store."

"It sounds as if you are staying on top of the home situation," I commented. "You are certainly to be congratulated on that account," I added.

"But I miss my Mother," Sarah lamented. "I wonder if she would approve of the way I am keeping the house."

I assured Sarah her mother would be very proud of how she was handling her role as woman of the house. Yet, regardless of the compliments extended to her, I sensed Sarah was still not fully convinced she was measuring up to her mother's expectation.

Turning the conversation around to the issue of her emotional burden, I remarked: "You definitely have had a lot of pressure settle upon your shoulders in the last month. Pressure enough to almost crush you," I added.

"I guess you could describe it that way," Sarah commented. Then with a flash of insight, she added: "Do you suppose those walls moving in on me have anything to do with my recently added responsibilities?"

"I think you have uncovered the source of your problem," I ventured. "The moving walls could be your brain saying you cannot stand any more pressure. Claustrophobia," I commented, "could be the sign you have assumed more than your brain can handle."

"There are times I think I can't handle all this responsibility," Sarah agreed. "But what am I going to do about it?"

I picked up on Sarah's quandary by suggesting: "It appears you are going to have to lighten up a little regarding your responsibilities. Speak to your Dad and work out a way that you do not have to cook as much. Also, have him take over the weekly laundry duty. Don't worry so much about the house cleaning. It doesn't have to be perfect as your mother kept it. Learn to relax a little regarding responsibilities." Sarah listened attentively to my suggestions and said we would talk more about this later.

When Sarah came in for another appointment, I commented that she looked a lot better than she had the week before. "Are you feeling better?" I asked.

"Yes," she said. "And you will never guess the reason."

"Tell me!" I pleaded.

Sarah began by announcing: "I had a dream or maybe it was a vision. In my dream, I was working in the kitchen performing my tasks and Mother walked in. She looked at me and said, 'Sarah, you are doing a good job. Continue to take care of your family.' Then she vanished and I found myself alone in the kitchen again. What do you make of that?" Sarah inquired.

I replied by asserting: "It doesn't matter what I think of it, Sarah. The real question is: How do you feel after having this dream?"

"I feel," Sarah declared, "Mother was validating what I am doing. All my feelings of coming up short regarding my housework are now gone. I feel really good about myself."

"Then the dream had real value for you," I said. "It was the validation you needed to convince you of your self-worth. I think you can go back to class after this recess and I doubt you will have any trouble with those walls moving in on you again. True to my prediction, Sarah returned to class the following week and had no problems.

****

"I don't like myself. I feel dirty all the time." The speaker of these statements was a young woman named Heidi, twenty-three years of age. Heidi had contacted me for counseling because she was experiencing deep depression.

I picked up on her line of thought by responding: "It sounds as if you despise yourself."

"Yes, I do!" Heidi emphatically replied. "I have a very bad self-image. Actually, I don't see anything good in myself. Even my dreams tell me I am bad."

"What do you mean?" I inquired. "Have you had a bad dream that distinctly told you that?"

"Well, I am not an authority on dream analysis but I am confident my last dream was saying I am a morally dirty person," was her reply.

"Please tell me the dream," I requested.

Heidi responded by relating she recently dreamt she was in a restroom. There was human waste spattered over everything. She was looking for a clean stall but couldn't find one. In desperation, she turned and walked out. At that point, she awakened. She concluded her remarks by commenting: "Doesn't that dream say I am a dirty person?"

Trying to be tactful, I replied: "You are probably correct in interpreting the dream as saying you are unclean. But that doesn't mean you are bad."

"Well, I feel I am totally bad," she lamented. "The other night, I picked up a bottle of sleeping pills and seriously thought about taking all of them. Then something within my head told me to get control of myself. At that moment, I realized if I was going to save myself from an early death, I had to get help. The next morning, I called you for an appointment."

Listening to her confession of desperation, I responded by rephrasing her desperation into relative language: "You felt you were on the brink of suicide?"

"Definitely," was her reply. "I need help or I most certainly am going to do away with myself."

Being confronted with her threatened self-destruction, I shifted my remarks to a supportive role. "In order to help you,"

I counseled, "I need to help you cope with your guilt feelings. You commented in our session earlier that you felt dirty all the time. That feeling was symbolized in your dream as a dirty toilet. In light of that revelation, let us begin with examining the source of the guilt that has been portrayed in your dream as feces spread throughout the toilet. It would appear to me you are carrying a lot of guilt for committing immoral deeds."

With downcast eyes, Heidi responded to my assessment of her situation. "You are correct. I have been living a very immoral life," she admitted. "I have had sex with numerous unmarried and married men. Each time it happened, I would tell myself I was not going to do that again. But I did. From my conduct, it seems apparent I cannot control myself. That is what scares me the most; I cannot control my own action. The only way out of my dilemma, that I see, is to commit suicide.

"Before you settle on that option," I advised, "let us look at your psychic self to see why you cannot control your sexual urges. To begin this inquiry, I would ask you a pertinent question: What do you acquire from sexual encounters? Is it pleasure, power, love or something else?"

Heidi thought about my question for a moment before replying. "I hadn't thought about it in those terms," she responded, "but now that you mentioned it, I would have to say it is not pleasure. Sex may temporarily feel good but once it is over, I feel like crying. The sex act actually leaves me feeling empty inside."

"So sex is not providing you with a great emotional high?" I queried.

"Certainly not," she responded. "And I don't believe I seek sexual partners to manifest power. I feel more like I am being used rather than controlling the situation."

Sensing that Heidi did not know her real motivation for her immoral conduct, I asked her a further question to aid her self-understanding. "Then what did you need from all those men you were involved with? You say it was not pleasure and it wasn't power. Why could you not be satisfied with just one man?"

Heidi pondered this question also a moment before replying: "I guess I needed acceptance. It makes me feel good when a man desires me. But as soon as our lovemaking is over, I do not feel secure within. Instead, I feel the need to attract another man to reassure myself that I am lovable."

"What you are describing," I concluded, "is a person who is on a treadmill, seeking acceptance but never finding it. You falsely believed making love with someone would provide you with acceptance. But once the physical act was completed and your male paramour walked away, you were back to square one regarding your emotional need. Am I correct in my analysis?"

"That's it," she admitted. "I was desperate for acceptance, yet I never found the fulfillment for my need."

"To help understand yourself further," I ventured, "you need to understand why you have this insatiable need for acceptance. In the normal development of a child, the child is assured of acceptance through love manifested by the parents. In your case, it appears there was a deficiency of love during your developing years. Were you not loved as a child?" I asked.

"I felt my mother loved me," Heidi replied. "But I never felt love from my father. Regardless of the good grades I brought home from school, or the work I did around the house, or new clothes I wore, Dad would never utter a word of approval. I can remember as a young teenager longing for Dad to give me a hug and tell me he loved me. But he never did." When Heidi finished speaking, she was sobbing with emotion.

I waited until she had finished crying and then attempted to bring insight to her emotional dilemma. "Could it be," I ventured, "that all your immoral conduct has been motivated by your desperate need to have a male figure accept you as a person?"

"I suppose that could be true," Heidi replied. "Certainly, I know I need someone to accept me as a person, not just my body. Yet even when someone said they loved me, I didn't believe them. I would go looking for another lover to verify I was lovable."

"That attitude of mind could cause you to prostitute yourself for acceptance, could it not?" I commented. "Yes, I can see that it would," she agreed. We went on and talked about why she couldn't accept as truth a man's profession of love. The conclusion we reached regarding Heidi's problem was tied to her father's lack of showing affection. In her mind, if her father did not consider her a beautiful person, how could any outsider see her as lovable? Thus, she was on a treadmill in her relationships with men, seeking something she was not emotionally able to receive.

We spent considerable time discussing the issues: love, acceptance, wholesome male images, and her self-image. Slowly but steadily, Heidi gained control over her interpersonal relations. Unbeknownst to herself, Heidi's wrong concept of the male species was modified by my acceptance of her as a person.

After lengthy counseling in which Heidi gained constructive insights, she raised an additional issue that required attention. "Knowing now why I have been sexually promiscuous does not solve my entire problem," she asserted. "I still feel dirty and hate myself for the things I have done in the past."

As a Christian, I understood where she was coming from. For one who has a conscience, moral misconduct results in guilt. Genuine guilt, as opposed to false guilt, cannot be removed by psychological counseling. All counseling can do for genuine guilt is to cover it with a rational explanation. Rather than removing the guilt, this method of disposing of guilt only buries it deeper in the subconscious. Real guilt is against the righteousness of God. To remove guilt, a person must receive Divine forgiveness.

Hearing Heidi's lament regarding her load of guilt for past transgressions, I voiced a message of hope. "It is not strange that you would raise the issue of guilt," I commented. "And I have good news for you regarding that issue. To help you, I must change hats. I wear two hats: one is that of a psychological counselor and the other one is that of a spiritual theologian. Speaking now as a theologian, I can advise you the problem of your guilt feelings involves forgiveness."

Heidi perked up at my diagnosis of her need and asked: "How do I obtain this forgiveness?"

"As a theologian, I can assure you God is a God who forgives. In the Bible, the promise is proclaimed: 'If we confess our sins, he who is faithful and just will forgive us our sins and cleanse us from all unrighteousness' (I John 1:9). What that means," I added, "is if you are truly sorry for what you have done and ask for God's forgiveness, you will be forgiven. That is the promise of God's Word."

We talked at length about God, sin, and forgiveness. After considerable discussion, she confessed to me, as a representative of God, that she was sorry for what she had done wrong. As God's representative, wearing my theological hat, I assured her of forgiveness through Jesus Christ our Lord.

Although she had confessed her sins and in Christ's name I had assured her of forgiveness, Heidi did not feel forgiven. She said she believed it, yet she had not experienced in her heart the joy of being forgiven. We wrestled with this problem for a couple of weeks in counseling. The problem was Heidi had never experienced on a horizontal level with another person the acceptance that comes when one is forgiven. As a result, she was having difficulty experiencing the feeling of forgiveness from God that was on a vertical dimension.

A few weeks later, Heidi came to my office all aglow. When I inquired regarding her happy countenance, she replied by informing me she had experienced a dream.

"Please tell me," I exclaimed. "It must have been wonderful."

"It was," she said. "It was basically the same dream I had when I first came for counseling. You remember," she remarked, "the dream regarding the dirty toilet. Well, this one was different. I was in a toilet again, but this time the toilet was spotlessly clean."

"So what does it tell you?" I asked.

"It tells me I have received Divine forgiveness," Heidi said. "This is validation for my belief. I now feel great!"

Heidi had experienced a breakthrough due to a dream. From there on, her progress was all uphill.

****

Validation is needed at every stage in life. Even in a nursing home, there are those who need the reassurance their thinking is correct. Only then will they enjoy peace of mind. An illustration of this transpired recently for a friend who was confined to his bed in a nursing home. Dr. John Calvin was his name and he was a retired medical doctor.

Dr. Calvin had been my personal physician for a number of years. He practiced medicine until he was seventy-five years of age. At that age, his mobility gave out and he was confined to his home under his wife's care. This semi-confinement lasted for ten years. During those years, Dr. Calvin pursued his hobby of writing. Eventually, his wife suffered a fatal heart attack one morning, leaving John alone. Not being able to care for himself, John had to be moved to a nearby nursing facility.

During his nursing home confinement, it was my custom to occasionally call on John. After our opening pleasantries, we would discuss his situation and subjects of mutual interest. Beyond his personal health issues, one subject disturbed him greatly. This involved his concern regarding the heavenly relationship he would share with his deceased wife. Each time we visited, John would bring up this concern.

The background of the problem related to the difference in religious thinking between John and his wife. He informed me he had enjoyed twenty-seven years of happiness with his beloved Thelma. Throughout those years, they had related well and enjoyed a good marriage. But regarding the area of religion, they had never reached a compromise. His wife, Thelma, was a member of a theologically conservative Protestant denomination. John, being a Presbyterian, was considered by her denomination a nonbeliever. As such, he was not permitted to receive Holy Communion in her church. John admitted he was as strong-minded as his wife regarding his denomination. As a result, throughout the years of their marriage, they never shared a union of minds regarding religious thinking. Due to Thelma's sudden demise, the issue was never resolved between them.

John was now lying in a nursing home facing his own death. As he meditated on the hope of life in heaven, the concern that troubled him was how would the two of them relate in heaven? He believed they would both be there. Yet because they had never been theologically in agreement during the years of their marriage, John wondered what their relationship would be in heaven. It was a frivolous question to others but a real concern to John. Unless he found some answer to that question, he would continue to face the future with trepidation.

In response to his dilemma, I tried to reassure John regarding life in heaven. "Marriage," I told him, "is not the same in heaven as it is here on earth. You will know each other but you will not share an intimate relationship." I quoted the words of Jesus: "In the resurrection, they neither marry nor are given in marriage, but are like angels in heaven" (Matt. 22:30).

"I believe that," John replied, "but it would be a great comfort to know my wife and I could be one in spirit regarding our religious belief."

We talked at great length about the relationship of couples in heaven. I shared passages of Scripture that spoke of the association between saved souls. All my line of reasoning could not relieve John's mind regarding his fear that Thelma and he would be eternally separated.

The next time I visited Dr. Calvin, he was bright and happy. I commented regarding his good mood. He informed me his dilemma had been resolved by a dream. Being happy for him, I asked him to relate the dream to me.

"I dreamt," he said, "Thelma and I were riding in a faith-mobile. It resembled a two-seated, open convertible that seemed to float along wherever we desired to go. Everything appeared heavenly around us, light and beautiful, and all was serene and peaceful. I thought as we rode along how wonderful it was that we were finally together as one. As we continued our journey around heaven, I awakened."

After listening to John describe his dream, I inquired: "What did the dream say to you? How do you interpret it?"

His reply was almost instantaneous. "It gave me validation my wish was going to be fulfilled," he said. "Now I am happy because I know we are going to be together spiritually in heaven."

Who was I to argue with John's interpretation of his dream? To John, his dream had given validation regarding the fulfillment of his wish. Finally now, he was at peace in his mind.

Chapter Five

-DREAMS-
REVEALING INNER SELF

Who are we? A sizeable number of individuals throughout our society could not answer that question correctly. That is not because they are deliberately lying, but rather because they are not aware of all the subconscious emotions that are moving them around on the chessboard of life. Counseling is the science that helps individuals become aware of those subconscious influences. As such, it helps emotionally crippled people become more open to reality and to responsible decision-making. Sometimes counseling alone will not unlock the door to stealth influences, which determine conduct. When that happens, the counselor may revert to dream analysis in order to expose the real self, hidden below the surface of self-awareness.

His name was Erick, and he was a successful salesman. Erick was forty years old and presented himself as a handsome, well-dressed gentleman. A year previously, he had requested me to conduct his wedding ceremony. It was to be his third marriage. I insisted on extensive counseling in preparation for his trip to the altar again. In our counseling sessions preparatory to the approaching wedding, issues that had led to the breakup of his two previous marriages were discussed. He ascribed the breakup of his first marriage to the immaturity of both him and his ex-wife. They had married young, right out of high school, he told me. After a few years of maturity, they discovered they were not compatible with each other. Their marriage ended with a mutual agreement to divorce and go their separate ways.

Erick indicated his second marriage ended because his wife withdrew her affection and caused him to live in emotional isolation. This marriage arrangement left both of them totally unsatisfied with their union. After a year of domestic isolation, Erick had filed for divorce.

Hearing the explanation of his marital failures, I attempted to help Erick understand himself in preparation for moving forward. We discussed at great length the emotional characteristics that enable an individual to share in a marital commitment. Assuming he was telling the truth, I had consented to perform his third marriage.

Now, a year later, Erick walked into my office for counseling. After a few moments of catch-up conversation regarding the major events that had transpired since his recent marriage, Erick informed me he was again divorced. Shocked at this disclosure, I asked him what I could do for him. He replied with a plea. "You have to help me," he said. "I have gone through three marriages. I could tell you it was the other person's fault, but that can't be true. There has to be something wrong with me to have failed this often. I need your help to find out who I am."

With that introduction to our counseling experience, we began to examine the characteristics of his personality and how they had contributed to conflicts in his marital relationships.

We discussed at length the problems in his three marriages. Regarding his last marital attempt, Erick informed me his relationship with his recent wife, Betty, had started out fine. After a few months, Betty began to upbraid him for household chores left undone. He responded to her criticism with silence that did not resolve the issues.

Hearing Erick relate how he responded to criticism, I commented that he sounded as if he were a passive-aggressive personality. He inquired what that meant. I explained how a passive-aggressive individual responds to conflict with silence rather than verbal argument. Erick admitted he had never raised his voice in self-defense. The result was that his wife, Betty, became frustrated because he would not verbally fight with her. As a result, issues were never brought to closure but temporarily buried awaiting resurrection during their next disagreement.

With loss of harmony in their marriage and latent anger resulting from unresolved disagreements, sexual feelings were blocked out, widening their emotional separation. Eventually, the emotional gulf separating Erick and Betty strangled any feeling of love they originally felt. The end result was a desire by both parties to divorce.

The next counseling session began with a leading question: "In light of your three failed marriages," I asked, "what has been going on in you? Or to say it another way, what has been the trigger that has shot down all three marriages?" Erick looked at me with a blank stare and said: "I don't know. That is why I am here. There has to be something in me causing the breakup of my marriages."

For a couple of weeks, we discussed together various personality traits that might have caused conflict in relationships with his successive wives. Arriving at no conclusive cause for his failed marriages, in desperation I changed the subject and asked: "Have you had any interesting dreams recently?"

"Strange that you should ask that," Erick replied. "I have had a recurring dream through the years. I dreamt the same dream again this past week. I know it relates to a bad period in my childhood but I don't see that it has any application to my present life."

"Tell me the dream," I requested, "and we will discuss later how it might be relevant to your present life."

"The dream," Erick began recounting, "has its setting in a schoolyard. A boy is one of the students on the playground. The other students are all teasing him about his pimples and red complexion. He can not stand their taunting so he walks away. As he does so, he walks past a group of girls, snickering and pointing fingers at him. He feels terrible as he passes them. Walking to the edge of the schoolyard, he stops and looks back. Another well-dressed boy approaches the cluster of girls and they dance around him with excitement. At that point in the dream, he awakens."

"What does the dream say to you?" I inquired.

"Oh, I think it is pretty self-evident," he responded. "It portrays my feelings when I was a teenager. I was teased a lot in school because I had red hair and a serious case of facial pimples. The boys teased me and the girls rejected me. I have always understood what the dream was referring to."

"True, you understood what the dream was referring to," I commented, "but did you understand how that experience affected your adult life?"

"What do you mean?" he asked.

"Well," I continued, "if twenty-five years later you are still having the same disturbing dream, then it stands to reason there must be a painful residual memory lingering in your subconscious mind. Such an emotionally charged memory is bound to have an effect on your normal daily activity. For you to be relieved of that pressure, you must expose the suppressed emotion and remove its influence over you."

"That sounds logical," he commented. "How do we do it?"

"We begin," I declared, "by looking at how the teasing of your childhood classmates affected your personality. For instance, how did you feel about yourself in light of their taunting?"

"They made me feel insecure," was his evaluation. "I was afraid to approach any group and saw myself as someone undesirable to others."

"You must have learned to cope with that feeling, for you now are a successful salesman," I commented.

"Yes, I did learn to cope with it," Erick retorted. "When I became an adult, I determined I was as good as any one of them and I would prove it. I bought a new suit, dressed myself up, went out and obtained a job. By strength of inner determination, I made a success of myself."

"You also dressed yourself up, went out and found a wife like the well-dressed boy in the dream," I volunteered.

"Yes, people respect you when you are well-groomed, and women will notice you," he commented.

"Yours was a great personal achievement," I remarked, "but in your subconscious mind, did you really feel self-confident out there in the business world?"

"No," Erick admitted. "Inside I always felt insecure but I never allowed anyone to see that side of me."

"So you have done a good job of hiding from people all these years," I ventured. "In your sales job, are you afraid to approach new customers?"

"No," he replied. "I can walk in and greet a potential customer without any fear. But I must admit, I procrastinate about responding to a complaint from an irate customer."

"You mean you are not secure enough inside yourself to accept criticism," I queried.

"I have always made an excuse for procrastination in servicing irate customers," Erick admitted. "Now that you have pointed out the significance of the dream, I can see my insecurity is still influencing my daily activity."

Hearing Erick admit that he recognized how his subconscious mind had been affecting his conscious daily conduct, I switched back to analyzing his marriages. "Regarding your failed marriages," I commented, "could it be true that you emotionally withdrew from your wives because they criticized you?"

"I suppose you are right in your evaluation of my motivations," Erick admitted. "I can't stand criticism because it reminds me of my youth. When I am confronted with someone's complaint, I just want to get away. I guess that is what happened in my marriages. After the honeymoon was over and there was a disagreement, I emotionally cut myself off. Once this happened, communication broke down between my wives and me. Eventually, we wanted out of the union."

"Your dream then is the story of your life, is it not?" I concluded.

"Yes, now I see the interaction," he admitted. "All these years, my insecurity has been tripping me up. I need to accept who I am and relate to others as a mature adult."

When Erick became aware that his daily conduct was being manipulated by his subconscious insecurity, he was able, with additional counseling, to make a basic change in his personality. After a period of time, Erick acquired another lady friend. He admitted to his new friend his past problem of insecurity. Due to his openness and honesty, the two of them were quickly drawn together in deep friendship. My last contact with Erick was the receipt of a 25th wedding anniversary card mailed from a distant state. Insight and honesty had resolved his insecurity problem and he was now living a normal life.

****

"I'm depressed and full of anxiety. I have difficulty functioning at my job." Those were the opening remarks spoken on the occasion of our first counseling session. The speaker was a young woman, in her mid-twenties, named Autumn. She made an appointment seeking help to straighten out her life. Autumn informed me she was married and worked as a nurse in a local hospital. She stated she did not know what her problem was, but she was experiencing emotional turmoil that was tearing her apart.

I began our counseling session by collecting background information regarding her life. Autumn related that she had been married three years. Her husband, Omar, was an Iranian immigrant. He had graduated from a local college and now worked as a policeman for their community. Both she and Omar were busy with their vocations and their time together was limited. Omar's work schedule involved the evening shift while Autumn worked days. As a result, Omar and Autumn did not see much of each other during the week. On weekends, their social life consisted of meeting with other couples at a local bar where they enjoyed drinking and playing darts. Autumn participated with the group but did not really enjoy herself.

After listening to her opening remarks, I asked: "Are you having marital problems?"

"No, I don't think that is my problem," she asserted. "It is true we have our differences, but we seem to be coping with those."

"What are those differences?" I inquired. "Tell me about them."

"Well, we don't enjoy the same recreation," she responded. "Omar wants to party with his friends and their wives. I would like to so something entirely by ourselves, but he is not interested in that. We have discussed this issue but have not reached a compromise."

"Did this problem exist before you were married?" I inquired.

"I suppose it did but I was not aware of it then. I was attracted to Omar because he was so outgoing, always partying and having fun. I was not accustomed to that lifestyle and it appealed to me then. Now, I am getting tired of it but he wants to continue to party every weekend. I would like to visit my family or go to the zoo or someplace different."

"If you had a child, your lifestyle would have to change would it not?" I commented.

"Yes, but Omar does not want to start a family at this time. He says we are too young to settle down to family life."

After listening to Autumn describe differences between her and Omar, I suspected there was a major difference that she was not admitting. In order to dissect the heart of her problem, I asked the leading question: "Are there cultural problems between you two?"

"Yes," she replied with sadness in her voice. "Culture is a real problem for us. Omar is a Muslim and I am Catholic. We were married by a judge. On religious holidays and festivals throughout the year, we have disagreements regarding how to observe them. Since we were married, I have postponed practicing my faith in order to maintain harmony in our marriage."

"That must build some deep resentment in you?" I commented.

"I hadn't thought of it as being resentment, but now that you mention it, I must admit I am resentful that he will not allow me to practice my faith," was her reply.

"In light of what you have told me," I added, "I suspect there may be a civil war going on in your head between what you 'ought' to do and what you 'are doing.' Certainly, you are living contrary to the teachings of your childhood. That kind of an internal conflict can cause all kinds of emotional as well as physical problems." Having said that, I then applied this truth to her personal life with the concluding statement: "Such an emotional conflict could explain the depression and anxiety you mentioned when you first came in for counseling."

My suggested diagnosis jarred her thinking and she paused a moment before speaking. "Perhaps you are right," she replied. "I feel like there is a civil war going on within my head. Let me think about that some more."

"While you are thinking," I added, "I suspect you will have a dream or two triggered by our discussion here today. Please write them down and bring me a report next week."

When Autumn returned the following week for counseling, she had a dream to report. She dreamt she was to meet Omar at a particular house for a party. When she arrived, the house was dark and empty. Entering the house, she saw dead bloody bodies all over the floor. The only living thing was her pet dog. As she searched the house, she sensed someone was there. Occasionally, she would hear the laughter of a man from somewhere out of the darkness. Eventually, she ended up in the kitchen where she crunched up in a ball in a corner and waited for the hidden person to get her. With overwhelming fear gripping her, she woke up.

"Does the dream make sense to you?" I asked.

"No," she replied. "But it certainly terrified me. I remember I woke up screaming."

"Let us look at it for meaning," I suggested. "Before trying to interpret it, we need to recognize that subconscious feelings express themselves in symbols during dreams. To understand the message of a dream, you have to interpret the symbols. Are you with me this far?" I asked.

"Yes," was her reply. "I think I understand your approach."

"Fine," I replied. "Now let us look at the first symbol. What was the opening scene of the dream?"

"I guess the first symbol was a house," she related. "I was to meet Omar at a house."

"Correct," I affirmed. "A house is where married couples live. In the dream, you and Omar were meeting at a house, representing your marriage. But if the house represents your marriage, what does the appearance of the house have to say about your marriage?"

"In the dream, the house was dark and empty," she replied.

69

"Yes," I commented. "This symbolism is descriptive of your life. Your marriage is not bright and happy, but it is dark and empty of companionship."

"So it is," she affirmed with a nod of her head.

"The next symbols in the dream are dead, bloody bodies all throughout the house," I commented. "Do those mean anything to you?"

"No, I don't understand that symbol," Autumn replied.

I let her dwell on that thought for a moment and then picked up the conversation again. "The dead bodies could not represent people. So let us think of something they could represent. What has died in your house, figuratively speaking...your marriage, since you two were married?"

Autumn thought about my question a moment and then replied, "I know the answer to that question!" she exclaimed. "It is my dreams. I had all those lovely daydreams of what married life was going to be like, and they are all dead."

"A wonderful diagnosis!" I replied. "But there was an additional insight revealed regarding the death of those dreams. In the dream, Autumn, you said those dead bodies showed signs they had died violent deaths, as shown by the fact they were all bloody." I paused to let her ponder that thought then added: "How many fights and arguments did it take to kill all those dreams?"

The recalling of the past brought tears to Autumn's eyes. She had fought desperately to acquire those dreams of young love but had failed. In her face, I could see that accepting reality was a heavy burden to bear.

Continuing on with our analysis of the dream, I added the statement: "There are still other symbols in your dream that we need to examine," I ventured. "For instance, there is the laughter of someone from out of the darkness. What could that laughter represent?"

Autumn thought a moment and then replied: "The only association I can tie to a laugh is Omar's conduct at our drinking parties. He is always laughing and joking around."

"I think you have interpreted another symbol in your dream," I said. "Although Omar's face is not revealed in the dream, the laughter in the darkness undoubtedly represents him. Sometimes the mind hides a person's face in a dream to protect the dreamer from too great a shock. In this case, I suspect Omar was hidden in darkness in order to protect you from the shock of the reality that he is your real problem.

"There is one last symbolic scene in the dream," I commented. "That is the scene of you crouching in a corner of the kitchen in great fear waiting for someone to get you. Do you see yourself in that picture?" I inquired.

"Most certainly," was her reply. "I see myself trapped in my house as chief cook just waiting for him to approach me. Yes," she continued, "I now see the dream is the story of my life."

"Dreams are always personal," I stated. "They are always revealing something about ourselves."

Autumn had made the connection with the message of her dream. It had revealed truth that had been hidden from her previously. Being now aware of this truth, Autumn had to determine what she was going to do with her newly-discovered insight. Counseling continued for some months as she attempted to sort out her true identity. Eventually, Autumn determined to seek a divorce. In her case, the Scriptural affirmation spoken by Jesus was verified: "The truth (insight) will set you free" (John 8:32).

****

"I don't feel any guilt!" That statement was spoken by a married professional man seated in my office. He had just confessed to being involved in an extramarital affair. His name was Jim and he was forty-five years of age. When he first

71

came in, I had asked him why he had called for a counseling appointment. His reply was that he wanted to discuss an issue that was troubling him. He related he felt torn two ways: he knew society would not approve of his conduct; nevertheless, he felt no remorse regarding what he was doing.

Hearing this confession as a counselor, I did not begin by telling him his conduct was morally wrong and he should stop his infidelity. To do so would not have solved his problem. It would only have motivated him to stop coming for therapy. The fact that he came for help revealed he had guilt feeling in his heart. My intent was to increase his awareness regarding why he had entered into a sexual liaison outside his marriage bonds. As a psychologist, I hoped to bring him to realize his course of action was destructive to both his marriage and his personal self-image. Also, as a minister, I believed Jim could not experience forgiveness unless he could feel inner conviction of sin. Therefore, I felt the imperative to help him recognize his guilt. Only when this awareness was acknowledged in his mind would he break off the adulterous affair.

I began the healing approach by asking: "Tell me the background of your indiscretion."

"Well, it happened by accident," he responded. "Neither of us ever intended for our relationship to move beyond that of mere friendship. Janet works in my office and we interact with each other professionally on a daily basis. Our first interpersonal contact was a dinner date we had while attending a company conference. That friendly encounter led to another. In a short time, we were meeting socially at least once a week. Janet had divorced a few months before and she felt she needed someone to share her inner feelings. I was willing to listen. After a few weeks, we felt a bond developing between us. Well, one thing led to another. Before we knew it, we were romantically involved. We sealed our bonding with sexual involvement. We are now one, we feel, and at this point we do not intend to change our present lifestyle."

Jim's calm rationale of his immoral activity overwhelmed me. This man, sitting before me, seemed to fully believe that his action was justified. "You really believe that you are not hurting anyone?" I inquired.

"No, I don't think so," he replied. "We are being very discreet about our association and I am trying to meet all my wife's needs. I will admit I wonder at times regarding myself. It doesn't sound logical, does it?" he said. "That is why I have come to you. I want to know if I am overlooking something."

The man's calmness baffled me. Jim appeared a refined individual and his background appeared morally sound. He asserted that he and his family attended church every Sunday. Yet in spite of his pretense of being a respectable Christian man, here he was admitting to a scandalous affair while maintaining he felt no pang of conscience.

I tried to prick his conscience by asking pointed questions. "What are you deriving from your affair?" I inquired.

"We are just complementing the need in each other's life," he volunteered. "She needs someone who accepts her and makes her feel good about herself. I need someone who accepts me as I am."

"Are you telling me your wife does not accept you?" I asked.

"Yes, she accepts me but she always has me on a pedestal. Through the years of our marriage, I never have felt she accepted me as a real person. I was always the person on a pedestal, but that was not the real me. Her approach always made me feel uncomfortable. Janet, on the other hand, knows I have feet of clay and still she loves me."

Although I had struck out with my pricking approach to his conscience, I continued: "If you don't feel guilt, what goes through your mind when you look at yourself in the mirror each morning?"

"I don't have any regrets," he boasted. "I feel I am handling everything in a balanced way. I am trying to be a husband to my wife on the one hand, and on the other hand I am providing Janet with what she needs."

"It sounds like you have convinced your rational mind you are justified to live the life you are pursuing, but I don't believe your subconscious mind agrees with that rationale," I commented. "If it does, then you have done an excellent snow job on yourself."

I directed a few other questions to him in the course of our counseling session. In each case, Jim responded with an answer that seemed to justify his conduct in his own mind. I knew that unless I could penetrate his rational mind, I could not hope to bring him under conviction and encourage him to change his lifestyle.

We concluded our counseling hour talking about the consequences if his wife discovered the truth regarding his affair. No consensus was reached regarding his conduct. Before returning the following week, I requested Jim to write down a dream or two that he might experience. He promised to try to document his dreams.

When Jim returned the following week, he came prepared to report a dream that was experienced a couple of days before. In the dream, he was on a trip somewhere. As he traveled along, he felt the need to go to a restroom. Turning in at a filling station, he went into the restroom. To his surprise, the restroom was filthy. In his words, "There was crap all over the toilet seat and on the floor." As he bent over the commode, his wedding ring fell into the crap. He pondered what he should do to retrieve his ring. Simultaneously, a voice behind him spoke, saying: "You had better clean that crap up." Hearing that command, he woke up.

It sounds like your subconscious is speaking loud and clear," I commented. "Before we start to analyze its message, let me give you a brief overview of how dreams are structured. Dreams use symbolism to convey their message," I explained. "Feelings and thoughts have no structure so they have to be depicted by some concrete form on the screen of the mind. This is the same principle conveying truth that the writer of an editorial cartoon uses in a newspaper. Once you understand the symbolism, you can easily deduce the message being proclaimed."

I began the interpretation of the dream by asking Jim if anything in the dream made sense to him. He replied the symbolism of the ring most likely would refer to his marriage.

"Correct!" I said. "The ring dropped into the crap most likely symbolizes your marriage. But let us go back and start at the beginning of the dream. I believe you said you were on a trip somewhere when you felt the need for a restroom?"

"Yes," he commented. "I was driving somewhere at the beginning of the dream."

"What do you associate with a trip?"

"Going somewhere," was his instant reply.

"Correct," I assured him. "You were going somewhere. Could that symbolism be in reference to life? In life, we are going somewhere."

"I will buy that," Jim replied. "The dream can be referring to my journey of life."

Once we had agreed on the setting of the dream, we proceeded to the next step in analysis. "What was the next symbolism in your dream?" I asked.

"It was the restroom," he volunteered.

"And what could a restroom symbolize?" I queried.

After a thoughtful pause, Jim responded: "Well, I guess you could say a restroom symbolizes that which you do that is personal."

"Personal, such as sexual?" I added.

"You could say that," Jim replied.

Our analysis was coming together so I pressed on with my search for the truth conveyed by the dream. "You said, I believe, the commode was all covered with crap. Would not that mean it was filthy with human manure?" I asked.

"Yes, that is how it appeared in the dream," Jim admitted.

"Why then did you call it crap?" I asked. "Why not use a dirty four-letter word instead?"

"I believe I know the answer to that question," Jim replied. "A friend at the office with whom I shared my secret a couple of months ago upbraided me by saying: 'Why don't you cut out that crap!' I still remember him making that statement."

I picked up on his mental association of that word regarding his conduct and said: "Your subconscious mind, it would seem, has chosen crap as a symbol to depict your immoral conduct."

"It appears that way," Jim admitted. "And I suppose my ring falling into the crap symbolizes the stinking mess my marriage is in due to my conduct?"

Leaning toward him across the desk, I administered the coup de grace with the statement: "I think you have just interpreted your own dream. The dream is expressing what your subconscious mind feels about your adulterous affair."

Jim sat in silence for a few moments meditating on what had been revealed.

Before he spoke, I administered the second coup de grace by asking: "What was the last symbolism of the dream...the last thing that happened?"

"You mean the voice I heard?" Jim asked.

"Yes, you said the last thing that transpired before you awoke was hearing a voice saying, 'Clean up this mess!' Was not that voice your inner conscience telling you to change your ways?" I suggested. "If so, do you still feel you are justified in what you are doing?"

Jim acknowledged he would have to do some serious thinking. I agreed he needed to do that and we set another appointment for the following week. When Jim came for his scheduled appointment, he showed signs of remorse. He finally conceded his action was not morally right. He hated to admit the relationship with Janet was dirty, but he acknowledged there were times when he felt unclean. We began to discuss how he was going to end the relationship. He admitted it would be hard but acknowledged it had to be done.

Counseling continued for a few months. My goal at this time was to help the client understand his actions and give him emotional support as he broke off the affair. Closure did not happen immediately because his will was weak. In spite of failures, he continued to struggle within himself. Eventually, Jim found the strength to become an honest man again.

During these final months of counseling, a few additional dreams were helpful in resolving his struggle and turmoil. Yet the first dream which we analyzed was the catalyst which started him on the road to recovery. In time, Jim became a devoted husband and father again.

Chapter Six

-DREAMS-
RESOLVING EMOTIONAL
CONFLICTS

When we are seeking help solving a personal problem, the advice frequently given by a friend is the statement: "Sleep on it!" Actually, that is not a trite statement. The fact is...the solution is probably already resolved in the depths of our mind. Our problem is that we have not yet been made aware of the answer. This is the point where dreams come into play. As we "sleep on it", the subconscious mind can reveal the answer through the medium of a dream.

"How can I help you?"

The question was directed to a middle-aged woman, seated across the desk in my office. She had introduced herself as Heidi, a married woman who worked as a secretary in a local office. Heidi appeared well-dressed, poised, yet delicate. While seated in a comfortable chair, her hands twitched with a nervous reaction.

Responding to my inquiry, she voiced her reply. "I really don't know," she responded. "I know I have a problem but I don't know what it is. I am nervous all the time. I can't sleep at night. I have difficulty concentrating at work. Sometimes I pick fights with my husband over issues that are ridiculous. I guess I would say I am a nervous wreck and I need help."

Heidi had described herself as a tormented, confused, unhappy person. Something was definitely disturbing her mind. It now became my responsibility to uncover the source of this disturbance.

I began our search for insight by asking what was putting pressure on her. Was she having problems in her marriage? I inquired. Were there personality conflicts in her office? How was she relating to relatives and friends?

In the course of our conversation regarding these questions, I learned that Heidi had a good marriage. Her husband, Tom, was very supportive. Being unable to help her himself, he had encouraged her to seek counseling. Tom's suggestion supported her assertion that there was no problem in their marriage.

Moving on from discussing her marriage, we talked at length about her relationship with co-workers in her office. Again, I could find no source of emotional pressure there. Heidi enjoyed her work and felt comfortable with her co-workers.

Next, our conversation turned to her extended family. Heidi informed me that her father had died a number of years before. Then two years ago, her only sister, Joyce, had died of breast cancer. In addition to that loss, her mother had died six months ago. "Now," Heidi said, "I am the last member of my family."

Listening to her relate the loss of two family members in the past couple of years, I felt definitely her present anxiety was associated with that loss. To explore my assumption, I asked the probing question: "How do you feel about the death of your sister and mother?"

"I have accepted their loss," Heidi answered. "I mourned each of them but in different ways. In the case of my sister, she suffered so much, I was relieved when she finally passed away. I could not wish her to continue suffering the way she was."

"And what about your mother?" I inquired.

"Mother was a different situation," Heidi commented. "She wanted to die. Age had taken its toll. She wanted to die and be with her daughter. I still remember standing at the foot of the bed the day she died. As she expired, I literally saw a ghostly spirit leave her body and ascend up through the ceiling. After seeing that transpire, I had no problem accepting her death."

We talked extensively regarding both of these deaths. Throughout our conversation, I could not connect Heidi's nervousness or anxiety to either of her loved ones' deaths. After a few weeks of analyzing events in her life, we appeared no closer to the source of her problem than when we began.

"The answer to your problem continues to elude me," I commented. "I am sure your subconscious mind knows what is troubling you. Let's hope that it will reveal the answer to you in a dream you might have this coming week."

When Heidi returned for her next appointment, she had a dream to share. "It is not what we hoped for," she remarked. "Actually, it was just a crazy nightmare."

"Crazy or not, let me hear it," I requested.

"In the dream," Heidi said, "I was in my house and there was a cat running around there. I picked up the cat and placed my hands around its neck. Holding it in this fashion, I squeezed its neck until it died. Once the cat was dead, I dropped it on the floor and awakened."

"That was a strange dream!" I exclaimed. "Do you have any idea what it was saying?"

"No," Heidi replied. "It certainly does not reveal my feelings toward cats. I have a pet cat and I love her. That's why I said the dream was just a crazy nightmare. It doesn't make any sense."

Before allowing her to discard the dream as pure nonsense, I attempted to direct Heidi in looking at the symbolism of the dream. "What emotion," I asked, "did the strangling scene of the dream express?"

Heidi thought on that a moment and then replied: "I guess you could say anger. Certainly, I was mad as I squeezed the neck of that cat!"

"OK," I responded. "If anger was what the dream was revealing, who are you angry at?"

The question drew a blank stare from Heidi. "I don't hate anyone," she responded. "I am not the type to hate people."

We talked about Heidi's feelings regarding people but made no connection between anyone and the dream. The dream certainly depicted subconscious anger, yet I could not discover the source of the anger. Heidi kept insisting she was not angry with anyone and could not understand why her dream was insinuating that fact. Being unable to ascertain its message, we dropped the discussion of the dream.

The next week, I was determined to pursue a new direction of discussion. Contrary to Heidi's assertion that she had no anger against anyone, my intuition told me there were negative feelings regarding her sister. It was only a hunch but it was worth exploring. In order to disguise my real motive, I suggested we talk about Heidi's childhood experiences with her sister, Sarah.

"You two were close in age," I commented. "How did you get along together?"

"Oh, we mostly played well together," Heidi responded. "Sarah was Mother's favorite but I didn't have much trouble with that fact."

Continuing our reminiscing of her early years, I asked: "Being close in age, did you double date as teenagers?"

"Yes, some of the time," Heidi replied. "But the older we became, the less that happened."

"Why was that?" I inquired.

"Well, when we went to dances, Sarah was always stealing my date away. I would meet someone I liked, and as soon as she saw us enjoying ourselves, Sarah would make a play for my boyfriend and dance away with him."

"Did that happen often?" I injected.

"Almost every weekend," Heidi replied. "When I would complain to Mother after we came home, Sarah would get mad because I told on her, and throw a fit. In her anger, she would come after me with her painted fingernails extended just like a cat."

"Eureka!" I cried out. "You have just explained your dream." With a blank look on her face, Heidi waited for me to continue. "Don't you see?" I said. "You just called your sister a cat. In your dream, you were strangling a cat. It appears the source of your anger is your sister."

Heidi's face changed color. Tears began to form in the corner of her eyes. With downcast eyes, she nodded her head in agreement. Finally, she spoke. "I have been angry with Sarah all these years. When she was dying, I couldn't vent anger at her because I felt sorry for her suffering so much. But I have never forgotten how she treated me when we were teenagers."

The source of her inner anger had been discovered. In light of that revelation, I attempted to drain off angry venom by prodding her to talk about how she felt regarding her deceased sister. Her words were like little ladles, dipping the hostility from the depth of her mind. After a few weeks of this therapeutic counseling, Heidi was free of the noxious feelings of the past. With the removal of this subconscious anger, Heidi regained her peace of mind.

****

Harry was a carpenter by trade. He built houses for his livelihood. Reared a Catholic, Harry became involved, together with his wife, Lois, in a small home-based discussion group, sponsored by a Presbyterian church. The group members shared personal problems and provided support and encouragement to one another. Through these small group dialogues, Harry became aware that he had some serious emotional conflicts in his personality. Due to this insight, he called for a counseling appointment.

When Harry appeared in my office, we began our session with the customary dialogue of introductions. Harry stated he had come because he had a problem. As a counselor, I knew better than to ask: "What is your problem?" If individuals knew their problem, they probably would not need to come for counseling. Knowing this, I continued our dialogue by asking: "How is your problem affecting you?"

In answer to that question, Harry began a description of his troubled life. "I do not relate well with people," he replied. "I feel they are out to hurt me. Actually, fear pursues me in everything I do. I am always imagining the worst scenario about every situation. This negativism affects my work and my business relationships."

"It sounds like you have an obsession with fear," I commented.

"Most definitely so," was his reply.

"Fear," I related to him, "normally has its beginning back in our childhood. How was your childhood? How did you relate to your parents?"

"Not good," Harry replied. "I believe my fear and insecurity can definitely be traced to my childhood rearing."

"Why would you say that?" I asked.

"Well, my folks tried to control me and my siblings by fear. I remember," he continued, "being threatened as a young child with the statement: 'If you go out of our back yard, wild animals will eat you.' As a child, I frequently would look through the fence for those wild animals."

"I bet you had nightmares because of that teaching," I commented.

"I certainly did," Harry admitted. "My fear in bed at night caused me to hide under the covers. Mother didn't know it, but it was fear of getting up in the dark that caused me to wet the bed for years."

"Was that the only fear your parents instilled in you?" I asked.

"No, there was another one which caused me to fear people," Harry commented. "I still remember my mother telling me if I wasn't good she was going to give me to the garbage men. One of the garbage men was black. That fear and the fear of wild animals gave me nightmares all through my childhood. I would wake up many nights in a cold sweat, shaking with fear."

"Are those fears still with you?" I inquired.

"Not in the same form," Harry responded, "but I still feel fear in many situations. For instance, I am insecure meeting new people, and I still don't like the dark too well. I have difficulty relaxing because I am always on the defensive, protecting myself."

After listening to Harry describe his childhood training, I realized he had been psychologically programmed with fear. Even though it was irrational fear, it still paralyzed aspects of his behavior years later. I explained this to Harry and challenged him to face his problem in the spirit of Franklin D. Roosevelt, who said at his first inauguration address in 1933 to a fear-conscious country: "We have nothing to fear but fear itself."

Proceeding on that assumption, I tried to help Harry analyze his fears and realize that they had no foundation. It was slow progress. Week after week, we would discuss situations that made him feel insecure. Once a fearful feeling was exposed, we tried to trace the fear back to its source. Slowly but steadily, our dialogues revealed the errors in his emotional building blocks.

After some weeks of reprogramming therapy, Harry reported a dream he had experienced. He dreamt he had gone back to the house where he had lived as a boy. In that house, there was a boy whom he perceived as his childhood self. Together, they were enjoying milk and cookies. The child was very scared because he had seen outside the kitchen window a black panther. Harry, the mature adult, asked the boy if they should invite the panther inside. The boy was scared to do that. After a while, Harry convinced the boy that they should invite the panther to join them in the kitchen. When the panther came in, the child found the big cat was just like a pet. The panther loved the milk and cookies. Harry felt wonderful when he awoke.

Hearing this dream, I exclaimed: "That is a fantastic dream! Your dream is revealing that we have made progress removing the fears from your subconscious mind."

"What do you mean?" Harry inquired.

"Well, look at your dream closely," I commented. "Your childhood fears were portrayed in the dream as a black panther prowling around your house. You, as an adult in the dream, reasoned with the boy to invite the panther inside for some milk and cookies. Once your childhood self did that, you found the panther was just a lovable cat who likes milk and cookies."

"I see what you mean," Harry said with a grin. "The dream was saying I no longer have the fears that have terrified me since childhood."

"That's right," I assured him. "We have made great progress in exorcising your childhood fears."

The next week, Harry had almost an identical dream. This time it was the same routine and the same result. In this dream, the garbage truck came by with the black garbage man. The boy was encouraged to invite the garbage man into his kitchen for milk and cookies. After the man came into the kitchen, the boy discovered he was a nice person and they became friends.

Experiencing these two dreams, Harry began to see changes in his attitude toward people and events. He became more self-confident and relaxed within himself. When negative thoughts would begin to fill his mind, Harry would remember the truth he had learned about himself. This knowledge gave him the power to cast off the dark shadows and live a happy, normal life.

****

To use a colloquial expression, she was running scared. Her fear was she would end up back in the State Hospital. The panic-stricken woman was Becky, a fifty year-old married woman with two daughters. Throughout her life, Becky struggled with bouts of anxiety. Two years earlier, anxiety had overcome her and she was admitted to the State Hospital. After six months of treatment, including shock therapy, she returned home to her family. Now a year later, her anxiety was returning. One symptom of her emotional disturbance was experiencing recurring nightmares. Becky knew if she didn't resolve these dream issues, she would end up back in the hospital.

Becky came to my office and voiced her concern. I requested she share her disturbing dreams with me. She was very obliging to do that.

According to Becky, there were two types of recurring dreams that kept disturbing her sleep. The first one was a dream involving her cousins. In this dream, she and her cousins were children playing together. They were swimming, running, or riding bikes. Always, Becky came in last in their endeavors, resulting in taunting remarks from the others. In the dream, she was always trying to catch up. Frustration and inferiority overwhelmed her as she played games with her cousins.

The second dream involved her sister and their social life. In this dream, Becky was always playing second fiddle to her sister. The sister got all the attention from relatives and friends while Becky suffered rejection on the sideline. In both dreams, the feelings and experiences she endured were very painful.

After sharing the two dreams, Becky continued by saying: "I don't know why I keep having these childhood nightmares. Although those experiences did happen, they have nothing to do with my present life."

"Why would you say that?" I inquired.

"Well, I haven't seen my cousins in thirty years. My mother had a family fight with my aunt, and our families have been separated ever since. The second dream relates to the jealousy I felt regarding my sister. That happened years ago also, and my sister has been dead for ten years. I don't understand how these two dreams could relate to my present life."

After hearing Becky's quandary regarding the significance of her dreams, I attempted to enlighten her regarding the structure of dreams. "The message of dreams," I assured Becky, "normally is not dependent on the characters portrayed in the mental pantomime. The characters in the dream are only actors who are portraying an emotion that is seeking to be expressed. The actor might be yourself or someone you know. Other times, the actor has no recognizable face. In some cases, the mind substitutes a different person for the one who is the source of a painful emotion.

" In your case," I continued, "you may have angry feelings against someone but not be able to admit it to yourself. Seeing them portrayed in a dream could be too shocking to confront. Therefore, your mind has reached back thirty years and picked up two situations involving ridicule and rejection portrayed by your cousins and your sister." I concluded my explanation by asking: "Do you understand how the mind can disguise the truth to protect you from pain?"

"Yes, I see how my dreams can be experienced in disguised form," she acknowledged.

."In light of that explanation," I suggested, "let us look at your dreams again. In the first dream, forget about the fact it was your cousins with whom you were involved. Consider, rather, the taunting and teasing you experienced in your encounter with them. In the second dream, your sister made you feel rejected and unloved. In both dreams, the actors and circumstances are different than your situation today but the feelings experienced, I suspect, are the same.

"Applying that insight to your present circumstances," I then asked, "is there any situation in your life today that is producing those same painful feelings?"

Becky was quiet for a long moment. Then with downcast eyes she replied: "I hate to say it but that is how I feel about my husband, Joe."

"Would you elaborate on that statement?" I requested.

"It seems," she continued, "like I am always trying to catch up to his expectations. He tells me to stop being nervous, to shape up, to forget the past. His constant criticism makes me feel very insecure, just like my cousins did." By this time, Becky was sobbing with emotion. After she regained her composure, she continued by saying: "He says I will be the death of him yet."

"What does he mean by that statement?" I asked.

"I guess he means I am so much bother, so upsetting to our family life, he might have a heart attack," she answered. "It all makes me feel so unwanted."

"It sounds like your husband is guilty of psychological abuse," I commented. "Does he recognize that he is a large part of your problem?"

"No," Becky replied, "he will not admit that he is doing anything wrong. I know he would not agree to counseling."

We talked at length regarding her home situation. I inquired if she had given any thought to a divorce. She replied that was not an option due to finances and her religious belief. In lieu of a divorce, I counseled, she would have to learn to cope with the situation.

The next few months of counseling centered on developing coping skills. I tried to strengthen her self-esteem so she could voice her opinions during arguments. Gaining new insight, Becky was able to disregard Joe's critical remarks. They still hurt but they did not devastate her anymore. She also developed a few social contacts with friends from whom she received affirmations.

After a period of time, Becky felt confident enough to cope with her home situation without counseling help. The nightmares were gone and she was courageously moving slowly ahead.

Chapter Seven

-DREAMS-
UNCOVERING GUILT

Guilt is a universal experience. The human psyche has a built-in awareness of right and wrong. When we act contrary to that inner standard, we experience feelings of guilt and shame. Even if these feelings are denied or distorted by our conscious mind, the subconscious mind will still convict us of wrong through the medium of dreams. Many emotional and physical problems have their source in suppressed guilt. In order to help individuals acquire a healthier mind and body, suppressed guilt must be exposed and resolved. Counseling is a prime method of accomplishing this objective.

"Hi! Great punch, isn't it?"

The speaker, Don Cook, was a fellow minister whom I had come to know casually through our area ministerial association. We were visiting around the punch bowl while participating in an interdenominational evangelism workshop. I jokingly replied that the punch had better not be spiked or he would be in real trouble with his conservative congregation. We joked back and forth and then moved away from the table to a couple of empty chairs.

Don and I had never talked extensively before, although it was common knowledge among the clergy delegates that I practiced professional counseling. On this occasion, he seemingly wanted to talk, so we chatted together for some time. It was not a serious conversation, although he became serious enough to ask if he could stop by my office the following week. After agreeing on an acceptable time, we split to mix with other guests.

In keeping with our agreed appointment, Don appeared at my study precisely on time. I asked what I could do to help him, and he replied he needed someone to help clarify his thinking.

"For some time," Don confessed, "I have been having real problems with certain doctrines of Scripture." He commented that as an ordained minister, it was assumed he was faithful to Christian teaching. Never had he admitted to anyone his lingering doubts. Now he wanted to talk about them.

Accepting his statement at face value, I began our dialogue by asking if there were any particular doctrines troubling him. Don affirmed that there were. Particularly, he had trouble with rules governing moral codes. He did not believe all drinking, dancing, card playing, and other forms of entertainment were morally wrong. The fact was, he had come to question God's moral law as taught in Scripture. Any conduct seemed to him permissible if done in the right spirit.

"What I hear you saying," I replied, "sounds like you have become a follower of the New Morality school of theology. In other words, you believe everything is permissible if it is done in the spirit of love."

"That's right," he answered. "I no longer believe in strict rules of right and wrong. Love, and love alone, is my sole test of any personal action regarding moral conduct."

I began to surmise there was more behind Don's remarks than he was openly verbalizing. Nevertheless, not wanting to close the door to further discussion by putting him on the defensive, I continued my probing very cautiously.

92

"That sounds fine," I responded with a smile on my face, "but you must have some doubts about it, or else you wouldn't have come to see me."

"I guess maybe I do," Don replied as he rubbed his hands nervously. "Logically, I can prove my point to my own satisfaction but inside I don't always feel at peace." We talked further about the need to sort out his feelings and to evaluate what he really believed. After agreeing to meet regularly on a weekly basis for a time, we parted.

When Don, arrived for his second session, he appeared to be in a talkative mood. He rambled on about the weather, church activities, and other miscellaneous subjects. I sensed he was attempting to keep the conversation from focusing on himself. After being outmaneuvered for almost fifteen minutes, I swung the conversation around by asking a direct question: "How has your week been? Any problems in your life?"

The question drew him back to our particular reason for meeting. "Remember what we talked about last week," he began. "Well, I saw a perfect example of it this past week. My wife and I rented the video, *Hawaii.* That film made me boil inside. The legalism displayed by those New England Puritan missionaries reminded me of my congregation. Their disdain for the human body and its normal passion was repulsive."

"You identified with the native Hawaiians?" I asked.

"Yes!" he replied emphatically. "Insofar as they were free from restraints. They radiated love in all their actions and did not live according to a restrictive moral code. Even their lovemaking was a free expression of their emotional feelings."

Listening to Don argue the case for freedom from moral restraints, I responded: "I am hearing you say you want to be free of moral restraint to do as you please. Maybe you would also desire sexual freedom to follow your passions," I volunteered.

"Oh, no! I'm not saying that," he retorted. "I just think you cannot draw a line down through life and say everything on this side is right, and everything on that side evil." As my friend kept bringing the conversation back to the subject of personal freedom of conduct, I surmised he was seeking to justify some personal action of his own. Further conversation at that time did not produce any admission of moral transgression.

In our third session, I determined to use a different approach in seeking truth. Since I had not gotten him to confess to any moral vices, I decided to seek the truth indirectly through his dreams. Believing dreams are pantomimes revolving around life's conflicts, I asked if he had experienced any interesting dreams recently. He readily responded he had. I requested he share one with me.

Don reported his dream was similar to the kind he experienced as a youngster. In this particular dream, some kind of demon or beast was loose outside his house. As the dream commenced, he was frantically hurrying around trying to get his family inside the house. No sooner had he gotten them inside and the doors locked, a giant beast started to break down the front door. One arm, covered with long hair, reached through the splintered door and tried to grasp someone. Don herded his family into the basement while the beast completed breaking through into the living room. As the family crouched terrified in the basement awaiting the next crisis, he awoke.

After listening to my friend relate this dream, I asked Don if he had any idea what it meant. He replied that he did not. To him, it was just a scary nightmare.

I explained to Don that dreams are always symbolic. Since a concept or emotion is without shape, the mind must choose a symbolic picture to make visible the feelings of the subconscious mind. Furthermore, dreams are letters addressed to oneself. This means the emotion expressed is how the dreamer feels within, not the emotion of someone else.

Based on these two concepts related to dreams, I asked Don to look again at what was the message of his dream. "What," I specified, "would you say was the basic truth being depicted symbolically in your dream?"

Don pondered a moment and then replied: "I suspect it is saying some force is seeking to destroy my home and family."

"Excellent diagnosis," I commented. "Symbolically speaking now," I added, "how far has this force progressed in destroying your home? Remember; don't let the literal details of the dream confuse you."

He replied that he understood my rationale and would have to say the dream revealed that his family's security had been destroyed by this evil beast.

"Since the beast which attacked your home was never seen," I pointed out, "it has to be assumed the beast was of a non-physical nature which could not be portrayed through symbolism in your pantomime." He nodded, indicating that he understood my explanation. I continued speaking. "Understanding this, we now come to the key question: What evil force, portrayed as a beast," I asked, "has been assaulting your life to the extent that it has nearly destroyed your home?"

I watched his face for the first telltale answer to my question. I was not disappointed. A flush passed quickly across his face. He started to say; "I don't believe I know of any," but my steady gaze stopped him in mid-sentence. After looking me in the eye for a moment, he continued speaking: "I suppose I would have to say it is the emotion of passion."

Observing that Don was reluctant to speak further, I projected a possible scenario. "It appears to me, Don, you are having an affair and the dream is asserting that the emotion of passion has almost overwhelmed your household."

With downcast eyes, he replied softly: "You guessed right. I have had a couple of passionate encounters with a married woman of my church."

After a moment of silence, I continued with a question: "How do you feel about your conduct?"

"The strange thing is," Don replied, "I really don't feel guilt-stricken. I know I should, but I don't."

"How do you explain that?" I inquired. "You are supposed to be a man of God. Yet you have involved yourself in sexual encounters with a married woman."

He hesitated for a moment and then replied: "I guess I have convinced myself no one was getting hurt. We felt drawn to one another and did what felt good."

"Isn't that just convenient rationalization?" I retorted with some disgust. "You know one of the commandments states: 'You shall not commit adultery.'"

"Yes," he replied, "but that is what I meant earlier when I said I am not sure I believe all the doctrines of the Church. I know the commandments, but I don't believe that commandment applies to me."

"How can you rationalize that line of thinking?" I asked with dismay.

"Because," he affirmed, "I believe it is the motive of the heart which determines whether one has broken the commandment or not. We love each other. We were not abusing each other. Therefore, I don't feel guilty regarding my action."

We talked the remainder of that hour about the implications of his action. For each argument I would raise, Don would respond with an argument based on love. His refusal to accept the Word of God as final authority made it impossible for me to bring him under conviction of sin.

At our next session, the Achilles' heel of his stonewalling defense was pierced. This was accomplished with the consideration of twin questions: First, what effect would your conduct, if it were known, have on your family? Secondly, could you continue in the ministry if your immoral conduct was exposed to your congregation? Those questions shattered his self-righteous thinking. At that point, he came under conviction of sin and broke down with sorrow. With sincere regret, he finally admitted his sexual acts had been wrong.

We prayed together while he contritely confessed to God his sin and pleaded for forgiveness. I assured him of the promise of Scripture: "If we confess our sins, he who is faithful and just will forgive us our sins and cleanse us from all unrighteousness" (I John 1:9). He now realized he must surrender his passion to the Lord and cease from further contact with his amorous partner. To strengthen his resolve, he promised to tell his lover he now realized his conduct was morally wrong and he would not be alone with her again.

Don's raging struggle within his soul played out in another dream. A few days after our confrontational meeting regarding his immoral conduct, he experienced another disturbing dream. In this dream, he walked into his church office to find a safe engulfed in flames. Inside the safe he knew there was much that was valuable. Observing the blazing flames, panic filled his mind because he felt everything in the safe was going to be lost. However, as the flames licked away at the outside of the safe, leaving untouched the inner contents, his feeling of panic was replaced with an inner tranquility. With that realization, he awakened.

After relating the dream to me, I inquired if he understood its message. He replied that he thought he did. "How do you interpret it?" I asked.

"I assume the safe symbolizes everything I cherish," he remarked, "my family, my ministry, the respect of the congregation. I am sure the flames represent my passion. At the beginning of the dream, I feared the flames of passion were going to destroy everything. That thought filled me with panic. Once I realized the flames were not destroying what was dear to my heart, I felt at peace."

"Why do you suppose the dream conveyed the message that you were not going to suffer loss?" I asked him.

He scratched his head for a moment and then replied: "It must be because I have confessed my sin to God and determined to obey the commandments. Certainly, that is 'the grace of God' which I don't deserve."

"I think you have correctly analyzed your dream," I remarked. "That is how I would interpret it."

I continued our discussion by commenting: "Assuming your interpretation of the dream is correct, you still have a serious decision to make."

"What is that?" he inquired.

"I am referring to the person of your wife," I replied. "You may have made your peace with the Lord but what are you going to do about your wife? Are you going to confess your unfaithfulness to her or not?"

The question shook Don's composure. How was he going to handle that problem? He admitted that he should confess to her his unfaithfulness, yet he feared her reaction toward him and the effect on her personal self-image. She had always considered herself less attractive than others. How would she feel knowing he had turned aside to another woman? Torn between two courses of action, he pleaded for guidance.

I informed Don that I would not make the decision for him. However, I offered to help him weigh the pros and cons of his dilemma. We began our consideration by discussing what would be the effects of confessing to his wife his infidelity. If his infidelity were kept a secret, everything in his life would appear to progress uninterrupted. Yet there was a downside to that secrecy. By not being honest with his wife, he would be forced to live with a hidden barrier between them. This barrier would prevent him from experiencing an emotional oneness of heart with her. Whether in dialogue or lovemaking, he would carry within a feeling of hypocrisy. That would be the price he would pay the rest of his life.

On the other side, if he told her about his unfaithfulness, there was the possibility she would not forgive him. Her frail self-image would have difficulty adjusting to the disclosure of his adultery. "Very likely," he asserted, "she would want a divorce." A divorce would have a domino effect on his entire life. His children would suffer great emotional trauma; he would be removed in disgrace from his pulpit; and financially he would be devastated. Paraphrasing the soliloquy of Hamlet, he faced the decision: 'To tell, or not to tell.' Much hung in the balance. There was no easy solution.

The final decision was not reached quickly. A war raged within his soul for weeks. I felt compassion for him, but I could not help him. Weekly, Don told me he spent much time in prayer over the issue. Over and over, we discussed the pros and cons of truthfulness. Always it came down to the question: Which decision would have the least damaging effect on people?

Four sessions later, Don announced he had reached a decision. His decision was not to confess his infidelity to his wife. I asked him if he felt he could live with that decision. "Yes," he said. "Especially since my decision has been validated by a dream."

I was shocked hearing of this surprise development, so I requested that he share the validating dream with me.

Don began by saying: "Two days ago, before retiring for the night, I reached my decision not to confess my adultery to my wife. After going to bed that night, I experienced a dream. In the dream, my wife and I were getting ready for bed. The bedroom window looked out upon a busy street. I tried to close the window curtains but realized, after getting into bed, people could still see in. Arising from my bed, I pulled down the blind. Instead of accomplishing what I intended, the blind ripped loose and fell to the floor leaving the window open to outside viewing. As I stood frustrated, surveying the situation, I noticed people on the sidewalk could not see in because there was a bush hiding the view of the bedroom from the street. Returning to my bed, I still felt embarrassed because we had no privacy. At that point, I awakened."

After listening to Don relate his dream, I was still puzzled regarding what message he derived from that dream. Therefore, I inquired: "What do you see in that dream which validates your decision?"

"Well, don't you see?" he began to say. "The bush protects my private life from public view. It is like in the story of Jonah. Jonah needed protection from the hot sun and the Lord raised up a bush to provide him shade. In my dream, the Lord provided a bush offering me protection from the stares of people on the street. I interpret that symbolism as validation for my decision."

I marveled at the analysis of his dream. Certainly, only a minister would interpret the symbolism of the bush as implying that message. Nevertheless, there was another message in the dream which he had not recognized. To complete the analysis, I said to him: "What does the ripping of the blind symbolize?"

He was not sure, so I offered a suggestion. "Could it mean your intimate life, symbolized by a bedroom scene, has now been exposed to view; to God, to me your counselor, to your amorous lover, and even to your inner true self?"

Don pondered my suggestion and then replied: "I get your point," he affirmed. "Yes, my life has been exposed publicly in that sense."

Hearing him admit to that insight, I added: "And the final message of the dream is the truth I related to you last week. You are going to have to live with that exposure the rest of your life."

With Don having reached his decision, we came to the close of our counseling sessions. He continued to serve his people with renewed awareness of the forgiveness and mercy of God. Although not obvious to others, the scars of his unfaithfulness remained in his heart. Always he was to remember that he was a sinner saved by grace.

****

Guilt sometimes disguises itself, even in dreams. Rather than being openly manifested through a normal dream, there are occasions when the message of guilt is hidden behind the apparent message revealed to the dreamer. Only careful analysis will detect this hidden second message portrayed through the dream medium.

An illustration of this occurred in the counseling case of Linda. Linda was employed as a representative for a multimedia company. Her job involved serving as a lobbyist with elected officials in Washington, D.C. Monthly, she was sent to Washington to lobby for legislation favorable to her employer.

The initial problem that brought Linda to my office seeking counseling appeared to be burnout. She was an attractive woman in her mid-thirties. Her pressure-filled life produced nervous strain so serious, she feared a nervous breakdown. Clearly it was evident if she did not learn better coping skills, she would need to terminate her present employment.

After preliminary discussion regarding Linda's situation and background, we began discussing areas where she felt pressure in her life. As we talked about her work and its effect on her life, it was apparent that her lobbying work was undermining her self-confidence. Slowly and steadily, Linda was losing faith in her ability to accomplish assigned tasks. With this loss of self-confidence came the fear that she was a failure. Fear, feeding on fear, resulted in her feeling burnt out. Listening to Linda describe the turmoil in her life, I asked the question: "What is the real problem with your work? I am sure you get paid well for what you do."

"Yes," she replied. "But the effects of my encounters as a lobbyist are taking a toll on me."

"Would you explain that further?" I requested.

"Well," Linda continued, "I go to Washington, talk to all those senators and representatives, and they treat me like trash. Many times, they will not grant me an appointment. When they do, they insinuate that I am a woman who doesn't know what I'm talking about. Can you imagine how that makes me feel? My self-esteem is slowly melting away."

"If I am hearing you correctly," I commented, "it sounds as if you are beginning to doubt your ability to influence people."

"That's right!" Linda responded. "My self-worth is up for grabs. I used to think I was somebody who could accomplish anything. Now I feel like a failure."

For the next few sessions, we discussed who Linda was as a person, listing her strengths and weaknesses. My goal was to build her self-esteem in order that she might cope with the rejection experienced during her interviews of those in Congress.

When Linda returned from her next trip to Washington, she reported having a dream while sleeping in her hotel room. It happened the night before returning home. Before retiring to bed, she had taken a friend to dinner. They ate a rich meal involving numerous portions of spicy foods. Later, when she retired for the night, her stomach was very unsettled. Due to the uncomfortable feeling in her stomach, she was not able to sink into a deep sleep. In her restlessness, she experienced a number of dreams, which she remembered.

One dream most vivid and disturbing, Linda related to me. She dreamt she was in a large banquet hall filled with a host of men and women. The men were maliciously assaulting the women, dragging them off to the side where they were sexually violating them. She, too, was assaulted and sexually abused by the men.

When Linda finished reporting the dream, I inquired: "What does the dream say to you?"

"I think I understand it very well," was her reply.

I gestured for her to continue, which she did. "The dream pertained to my frustration as a lobbyist," Linda remarked. "The malicious conduct of the men in the dream illustrates, I believe, how I feel regarding the conduct of those men in

Washington toward me. To them, I am just worthless trash. The dream," Linda concluded, "was an expression of my inward feeling of being used and discarded by public officials with whom I work."

After listening to Linda relate what she perceived to be the message of her dream, I agreed she was probably right in her interpretation. That was undoubtedly the immediate message of this dream. "However, I believe," I commented, "your dream has another message even more personal than the message you have just described."

Somewhat surprised, she inquired: "What are you talking about?"

"Before I express what I believe is the second message hidden in your dream, let me explain how dreams are formulated by the mind. Once you understand the construction of dreams, I believe you will recognize the second message being delivered by this nocturnal movie."

I explained that dreams not only reveal subconscious struggles and issues which disturb us, they also frequently throw light on past feelings and experiences. This is almost an unavoidable relationship. The interaction is due to the fact that emotions in their original state do not possess form. Love, hate, anger, frustration, etc. are all devoid of physical reality. If you were to express them on canvas or as a picture, it would be necessary that you paint some scene portraying the inner emotion that is non-physical by nature. To display hate for instance, you might draw a picture of one man beating another man over the head with a club. The act of clubbing would not be hate itself, but it would depict the emotion of hate.

Pausing to make sure Linda was comprehending the information I had imparted, I then continued my explanation regarding how dreams are structured. "Since the mind is limited to the use of pictorial scenes in order to express feelings," I said, "it has to reach back into the file of past memories in order to choose pictures that will portray the emotions welling up from the subconscious into the conscious mind. This necessity explains the logical connection between the present application of a dream and the symbolism used to convey its message. Since the mind is limited largely to its own archives of past memories for props used on the stage of the mind, normally we can discover additional insight regarding subconscious feelings by analyzing carefully the symbolism that is used.

"Having said all that," I added, "now we return to what I was talking about earlier. To learn the second message of your dream, we have to look at the symbolism used to convey the primary message regarding encounters in Washington. What was that symbolism?" I asked.

Linda readily answered my inquiry. "It was a mental picture of men assaulting women sexually," she replied.

"Correct," I answered. "And if your mind was limited in choosing from its archive some past memory of personal experience to display its message, from what did it derive that symbolism?" I queried. "In other words, have you personally had experiences of being sexually used and then discarded by men?"

The question shook Linda's composure. Tears began to well up in her eyes and she sat stunned before me. I paused for a moment and then continued to speak. "I know your anxiety has been aggravated by the rejection of officials in Washington but I also suspect part of your problem relates to guilt and disgust regarding your own personal conduct."

It was a long moment before she replied. Then with a tremor in her voice, she admitted that what I said was true. She had been involved with a number of men who had dumped her after the novelty of the sensual experience had passed.

Linda had a problem coping with rejection from congressmen. But she also had a problem resolving her suppressed guilt. Unless she could experience forgiveness for her past conduct, she could not regain a healthy self-image. Wearing my second hat as a theologian, I was able to reassure her of God's forgiveness and reconciliation. After extensive counseling, Linda regained her self-confidence and continued in her chosen occupation.

Chapter Eight

-DREAMS-
PRODING US TO BE
HONEST

"You know better than that!" someone will say to us. But the fact is, we may not know better in our conscious mind. The subconscious is another matter. Truth is known there. Our problem is that sometimes the conscious mind does not desire to know the truth. The truth might make us look foolish, guilty or immature. Therefore, the conscious mind places a filter on the subconscious, preventing certain truth from being brought into consciousness.

The subconscious mind, however, will not be stymied. Being restricted in revealing truth to the inquirer, the subconscious mind uses the subtle method of exposing forbidden truth through the medium of dreams. One way or another, truth known deep within our mind is made known to the dreamer.

It was an unconventional counseling experience. I had been invited to be the after-dinner speaker at the Women's University Club in a neighboring city. The assigned topic was Dream Analysis. Upon arriving at the banquet hall, I discovered I was an hour early. After apologizing to the program chairperson, I volunteered to wait in a side room until my appointed time on the agenda. The program chairperson, Gwin Moore, volunteered to wait with me.

We chit-chatted for a few minutes regarding common concerns. Gwin then presented me with a request. She informed me that a friend had experienced a disturbing dream recently and would appreciate hearing my interpretation of it. I politely replied that I was not accustomed to analyzing the dreams of strangers. "Good analysis," I commented, "requires that I know the general background of the dreamer." In light of the fact that her friend and I were total strangers, I did not feel I could fulfill her request.

Gwin would not take no for an answer. She continued to insist that I must give her my opinion regarding the meaning of her friend's dream. Her persistence wore me down, so I agreed to share with her my first impression regarding the dream.

Before sharing the details of the dream, Gwin gave a brief background regarding her friend. "This friend," she related, "was involved in cults. She participated in séances and tarot readings." After that brief introduction to her friend's lifestyle, Gwin shared with me the elusive dream.

In the dream, Gwin said, my friend and her husband were going to a séance. This meeting was being held upstairs in a remote farmhouse. After the couple had ascended the stairs within the house, they entered a dimly-lit room. Ten couples were gathered in that second-story room around a table. Lying on the table was the body of a dead man. As the séance progressed, the dead man began to show signs of life. While the assembled group watched in awe, the body on the table sat upright. My friend, Gwin said, grabbed her husband by the arm and pulled him down the stairs and out the front door. When the couple was safely away from the house, the dreamer awoke.

"That was the dream," Gwin announced. "What do you make of it?"

I thought about what Gwin had told me for a moment before replying. After a pause, I spoke. "Not knowing your friend," I remarked, "I can only venture a guess regarding the message of the dream."

"Well, what is your guess?" Gwin queried. "My friend does not see any message in it and she begged me to inquire regarding your interpretation."

Again, I felt pressured to do something I did not feel comfortable doing. Nevertheless, to please Gwin, I offered my initial impression regarding the message of the dream.

"I could be mistaken," I commented in beginning my analysis, "but I believe the dream is saying that in the past, your friend had an adulterous affair which is now dead. This is portrayed by the symbolism of the dead male body on the table. Most likely it was with one of the husbands in the assembled group. The fact that the location of the body was hidden away upstairs in a remote farmhouse would insinuate it had been a secret affair. Next, as your friend observed this body, it started to come to life by sitting upright on the table. This symbolism to me implies your friend is contemplating a second affair. Not wanting her husband to know of her unfaithfulness, she hurries him out of the house to protect herself. Then she awakens."

As I finished my interpretation of the dream, I watched Gwin's face. Shock and fear swept over her countenance. Why did I perceive that the imaginary friend she was describing was in actuality, Gwin herself? Even though I did not know what the truth was, my inner vibes told me. Without admitting personal involvement, Gwin continued the charade by speaking further regarding her friend. "I think you are right," she commented. "My friend confided to me some months ago that she had just broken off an affair. Then last week, she confessed to me she was thinking of becoming involved with another man."

Not wishing to miss an opportunity to help someone avoid a destructive pattern of conduct, I added an additional comment. "I would hope," I confided to Gwin, "you would tell your friend her subconscious mind is telling her to avoid the consequences of her immoral choice. The fear she felt in the dream regarding her husband's possible discovery of her unfaithfulness should give her pause before proceeding with her sensual venture."

Our conversation was cut short at this point by the call of the club president to begin my address. Gwin or her friend, whichever the case might be, had been prodded by the dream to examine the consequences of her action. Whether the prodding was beneficial or not, I never knew.

****

Society would label him a loser. The son of a professional couple, at age nineteen, Neil had flunked out of college because he wouldn't apply himself to study. While still living at home, he worked at a local McDonald's restaurant flipping hamburgers. His main interest in life was following sporting events and goofing off with his friends. Under the threat of being expelled from his parents' house, he came for counseling.

When Neil appeared for his first counseling session, he swaggered in. Flopping down on a chair, he assumed an air of indifference regarding the counseling ordeal. After the introductory comments were exchanged, I spoke directly to his flippant attitude. "I sense you are not happy about being here today," I commented.

Neil rolled his eyes, together with a smirk: "Yeah, I guess you could say that," he drawled. "The folks told me I had to come, so I'm here."

"You don't recognize any problem in your life?" I inquired.

"No, not really," was his reply. "I guess I am not much of a success in life but I am happy with who I am."

"What do you really enjoy doing?" I asked.

"Well, to begin with, I don't like to be confined to a job. I like to go to ball games, hockey games, football games, any game. And when I am not going to a game, I like hanging out with my friends."

"It sounds like your desired lifestyle requires the need of a considerable amount of money," I commented.

"Yeah, that's my problem," he admitted with a guilty look. "What I like to do costs money but I don't like to work where I have to take orders from someone."

"Sounds like you are on the horns of a dilemma," I replied. "What you like to do costs money but to get money you have to assume the responsibility of mature behavior." I paused for a moment, hoping he would hear what I had said. Instead, he continued the illogical rationale of immature thinking by adding, "I would like to have a sports car but Dad says he will not buy me one until I finish college."

"Do you think your dad is right in his judgment?" I inquired.

He paused a moment and then replied: "Maybe so, but why should he deny me the pleasure of a car when he can afford it?"

"Perhaps he loves you too much to keep you dependent on him," I volunteered. "I am sure he wants you to learn to be responsible for your own actions and become a mature, responsible man."

Although I had challenged Neil's thinking, I had not convinced him his logic was immature. Two more sessions of counseling did not resolve the issue. He still did not recognize an immature attitude was his problem. At the conclusion of our third session, I challenged him with a new idea.

"Neil," I said, "for the past three weeks you and I have been sparring with one another. You have not been willing to admit you need to change your attitude toward life; and I have not been able to illuminate you to your problem. Let me make a suggestion. Disregarding what your parents or I might think you should be, would you be interested in knowing what your subconscious mind thinks about you?"

"Yeah, I would like to know that," he ventured. "But how can we know?"

"Your dreams can reveal your true self to you," I assured him. "Keep a journal of your dreams this coming week and we will analyze them when we meet again next time." He agreed with the suggestion and we parted.

The next week, when Neil came in for his appointment, he had his notepad with him. On it, he had recorded an interesting dream and was ready to share it. "I am going to be interested in what this dream reveals about my true self," he commented. With that statement, he began to relate the details of his dream.

Neil dreamt he was president of a million-dollar corporation. He was in his office and was filling a large satchel with bundles of cash he had secretly stolen from the firm. After stuffing the satchel with stolen money, he walked out into the front office and chatted with the secretary. She interpreted his nervousness as a sign of affection and came out from behind her desk toward him. Neil backed off before her approach while she continued to pursue him around the office. Just then, his accountant came into the office. The accountant started to pursue the secretary and Neil began to pursue the accountant. Finally, Neil came to realize that was silly, so he went back into his office and picked up the stolen money. Carrying it down to his car, he locked it in the car trunk. As Neil got into the car to start it, he heard a hammering on the trunk lid. He rolled up the windows to block out the noise. All the windowpanes appeared to be thick and tinted black. Before he pulled away from the curb, a man dressed as a chauffeur took an ax and smashed out the windshield. Then he awoke.

When Neil finished sharing his dream, he waited for me to respond. After a short pause, I commented. "This dream is revealing more of your inner self than you might want to know," I said.

"What do you mean?" asked Neil. "I think I am ready to know myself."

"OK," I concurred. "Let's look at it section by section because I see it falling into three parts. The first section opens with you being portrayed as the president of a million- dollar company. In the dream, you are in your office, stealing bundles of cash from your own company."

Neil interrupted me by remarking: "That doesn't make any sense. I am not president of a company and I have not stolen any money."

I responded to his objection by commenting: "Dreams," I said, "use symbolism to depict truth. The symbolism that you are the president of a million-dollar company is portraying the fact you have great potential wealth. Yet this potential wealth is being stolen. Do you see that picture depicting you?" I asked.

"No," he answered. "I don't see myself in that picture."

"Well, let's look at it another way," I suggested. "You have great potential. You are intelligent. You could attend college and make something of yourself. Yet all this potential is being stolen by your laziness and rebellion again society's standards. Now do you see where you fit into the first scene of your dream?"

"Yes, what you say is probably true," he muttered softly.

"OK," I continued, "let's look now at the second scene. This scene involved the secretary pursuing you around the office and you pursuing the accountant. This section of the dream is saying something you are not going to want to hear."

"Go ahead, Doc," he responded with some arrogance. "Lay it on me!"

Given approval, I continued my analysis. "It appears," I remarked, "you have some latent homosexual tendencies. You tried to avoid the approach of the secretary while being drawn to the male accountant. Does any of that ring true in your life?" I asked.

I noticed Neil drop his eyes and catch his breath. Body language revealed to me there was some element of truth in what I had just said. After a long pause, Neil responded to my question.

"For some time," he admitted, "I have suspected I had some abnormal desires. I have never acted on them but I know they are there."

This subconscious fear was probably part of the reason he was rebelling against normal standards of society. We discussed at some length the implications of his sexual orientation. No final conclusion was arrived at but Neil appeared to have some latent tendencies to be sexually aroused by his own gender. Considerable additional counseling, I realized, was going to be needed in order to help him understand and accept his sexual orientation.

Eventually, our conversation returned to considering phase three of his dream. In this section, Neil was attempting to drive away with the stolen cash. As he prepared to leave, there was a hammering sound that he tried to block out by rolling up the dark-tinted car windows. When he prepared to pull away from the curb, a man dressed as a chauffeur took an ax and broke out the windshield of his car.

"This last section of your dream," I informed Neil, "is most revealing because it describes how you have tried to handle your problem and where you are now in overcoming it." Seeing the blank expression on his face, I knew Neil did not comprehend my interpretation, so I continued with my analysis.

"Locking the money in the car trunk and trying to drive away is portraying your present attempt to continue your lifestyle. The money represents your wasted opportunity and the car symbolizes your forward movement through life. But if you notice in the dream," I commented, "before you can get started, there is a hammering sound behind you. You respond by rolling up the windows to block out the sound. I interpret that scene in the dream as the criticism you have received from your parents. Not wanting to hear their advice, you have tried to block them out by erecting a barrier. Although that has been partially effective, Neil, as you began to drive away from the curb, someone dressed as a chauffeur takes an ax and breaks out the windshield of your car. Then you awaken.

"This scene, Neil," I emphasized, "is where I come into your dream. If the car represents your forward movement through life; and if the hammering on the back window is your parents lecturing you; then the chauffeur represents me. Why me, your counselor, you might ask. Because I am supposed to help people move ahead through life more freely, pictorially speaking...drive them like a chauffeur. Your mind has picked up that symbolism to represent my help in guiding you forward. To further explain the uniqueness of my being represented as a chauffeur, notice what I did. Rather than driving your car, which I couldn't do because the car represents your individual life, I break out your windshield so you can see more clearly where you are going. My challenging questions have been the ax to break through your protective tinted windshield. As such, my questions have brought you face-to-face with reality. At that point, the dream ends because you have not progressed any further forward."

Having completed my analysis, I waited for Neil to comment. Eventually, he spoke. "I guess my subconscious mind knows a lot more about the real me than I thought," he admitted. "But what do I do with all this knowledge?" he asked.

"That is the sixty-four dollar question!" I replied. "Now you know much more about yourself. What you do with this information will either make you or break you. The choice is up to you."

Neil chose to move forward in changing his lifestyle. I found him to be a good client who was open to self-analysis. With each successive counseling session, I was aware of changes in his priorities of life. The following fall, he enrolled in college and began the process of equipping himself for a productive future. With his dropping of a rebellious negative attitude, reconciliation was soon experienced between him and his parents. Neil was now on his way to becoming a mature, responsible adult.

****

She was a single person twenty-four years of age. Her name was Della and she lived with her widowed mother. Della had sought counseling because her anxieties were causing her sleepless nights, frequent headaches, and occasional spells of colitis. She readily admitted she had a problem and desperately wanted help resolving it.

We began our counseling by discussing her background. Della was an only child born when her parents were almost forty. She had few playmates during her childhood years. The majority of her time was spent interacting with her mother because her father had been a traveling salesman who was home only on weekends. Following his death in his mid-fifties due to a heart attack, Della lived alone with her mother. After completing two years of college, lack of finances for school forced her to seek employment. Throughout her student years, Della had been overprotected by her mother, thus limiting her social contacts with men.

After gathering the background information regarding her life, I asked Della the leading question: "What do you see as your problem?"

"I don't know," she replied. "I feel I am suffocating but that doesn't make any sense. I am a free person. I can do as I please, yet I don't know what I want to do. I have great insecurities about the future. For instance, if something were to happen to Mother, I don't know what I would do."

"It appears to me," I commented, "you have not been accustomed to making decisions on your own."

"It's true, I have never been completely independent," was her reply. "As a result, when I am faced with a decision, I panic. Today, I am panicky about a stressful situation coming up in my life at work. I met a man who I think is going to ask me for a date, and I am scared to death he might. That fear only increases my anxiety. With the increase of anxiety, I experience more colitis problems. It has become a constant merry-go-round for me."

"With your insecurity and anxiety," I commented, "you must have terrible nightmares."

"Oh, most certainly!" she exclaimed. "Most of my dreams are scary. I awaken from dreaming feeling panicky and then have trouble falling back to sleep."

"I believe," I remarked, "your dreams can tell us much concerning the source of your anxiety. Why don't you write down some of your dreams and let us analyze them together. I believe this procedure will help you overcome your internal stress." Della accepted my suggestion and came to her next session prepared with a documented dream she had experienced the past week.

As the dream began, she reported, she was in a cave. In this cave, there were drawers, as in a morgue, which could be pulled out from the wall. She examined these drawers one by one and they all contained dead bodies. One of the drawers she pulled out was marked Jesus Christ. After viewing the dead body of Jesus, a hippopotamus came into the cave. It told her it was going to kill her. Della ran outside where there was a picnic area with tables. The hippopotamus followed her outside and laughingly reminded her she could not escape. She awakened terrified at the thought she could not get away.

"That certainly was a strange dream!" I exclaimed. "It had to be scary for you to experience it."

"It certainly was!" she responded. "I awoke in a cold sweat and couldn't go back to sleep for a long time."

"Well, let us analyze this dream and see if we can discover any beneficial insights in it," I suggested. "To analyze it, remember, just as words are the means of communicating between two minds, so mental pictures displayed in dreams are the vehicle which relates a message to the dreamer from the dreamer's own subconscious mind. Do you understand what I am saying?" I asked.

"No, I am not sure," Della responded.

"Well, think of it this way," I continued. "In communication, when the vocabulary words used are known, the flow of ideas is possible between two people. In dream analysis, when the picture symbols are understood, the message from the subconscious can be interpreted. In your case, as we analyze the symbols used in your dream, you will come to know your true self, which I suspect you have been hiding from your conscious self."

"OK, I think I understand now what you are saying," Della replied. "Let's begin the analysis."

"All right, what is the first picture symbol?" I asked.

"I believe the answer to that is a cave," Della responded.

"Correct," I replied. "And what would a cave represent?"

"I don't know," Della answered. "I guess you could say it represents being confined or closed in."

"I think you interpreted that correctly," was my reply. "That description parallels how you felt when I first talked to you. Remember, in describing how you felt, you said you were 'suffocating'. Being in a cave is like being confined or suffocated."

Having determined the setting of the dream, I inquired regarding the next symbolism used in her dream language.

"The second symbolism was the drawers which pulled out from the wall filled with dead bodies," Della stated.

"Correct," I answered again. "Now remember, dead bodies represent something that were alive but are now lifeless. As symbolism, these bodies do not have to be physical bodies per

118

se." Having explained the mechanics of symbolism, I proceeded forward with a question. "What," I inquired, "have you lost in your life that is now dead?"

Della could not answer that question so I ventured a guess for her. "Being confined to your home and mother, have you given up on any specific goals?" I inquired.

Hearing my suggestion, her face brightened up with excitement. "Yes!" she cried out. "I have had a number of goals which have ended up dead." She then continued by saying: "At different times in my life, I have wanted to be an airline stewardess, a schoolteacher or a model in New York. Always, my mother would say I couldn't leave home or it wouldn't be safe for me to go out into the world on my own. Now, those dreams are all dead. Do you suppose that is what the drawers filled with dead bodies in my dream were representing?"

I nodded approval to her question. Certainly, her dream had revealed truth she had not been aware of before. Continuing our analysis I commented: "Now considering the drawer that contained the body of Jesus, this symbolism appears to be revealing a different message to you. Why," I asked, "would one of the drawers contain the dead Jesus?"

Della pondered over that question a long moment before replying. "I suspect," she finally alleged, "it must have something to do with my father's death. Before Dad died of his heart attack, I was faithful in church attendance. But once he died, I was angry with God. I said He could not be a God of love since He separated a father from a daughter who loved and needed him so much. Since Dad's passing, God has been dead to me. But I don't know why God would appear in my dream as a dead Jesus?"

"That is easy to explain," I ventured. "God is a spirit and has no form. To give God a physical form which could be symbolically displayed in your dream, your mind had to substitute Jesus, who was God in human form."

"Very logical!" Della marveled. "What you are saying is my mind substituted a tangible form for a spiritual concept."

"That is how the mind works," I assured her. Continuing our analysis, I directed her attention to the next symbol that was the hippopotamus. "What could that symbol represent?" I asked.

Again, Della was stumped and I had no ready answer for her. "I'll need your help on this one," I commented. "Maybe together we can discover its meaning. To do so, tell me what comes to your mind when you think of a hippopotamus."

"That's easy to answer," Della answered. "When I picture a hippopotamus I think of an animal, big and fat."

"Well, forget about the concept of an animal," I responded. "In dream language, the symbolism of a hippopotamus is not referring to any animal but is expressing a truth regarding someone or something. Since the mental picture of a hippopotamus suggests the word big or fat, what is associated in your mind with those words?"

Della thought on that question a moment and then enlightenment flashed across her face. In a state of shock she replied: "When I think of fat, I think of mother. Since Dad died, all she does is sit around and eat. I am disgusted with her size and have told her that many times."

"There is your hippopotamus," I commented. "And the scene in the dream where she said she was gong to kill you ties in with the dead bodies in the wall drawers. Your mother is slowly killing you, is she not, by destroying your goals and expectations?"

Della clinched her hands and dropped her eyes. The truth revealed was a shock to her thinking. In silence, she sobbed softly to herself.

After a pause, she spoke again. "I think I can interpret the rest of the dream," she responded. I nodded approval so she continued to speak. "My running out of the cave into a picnic area symbolizes my desire to enjoy life. I love the out-of-doors and enjoy being surrounded by scenes of nature. Yet even in the locations I love, my mother is still there and will not let me escape. That realization terrifies me, which was what I felt when I awoke," she concluded.

Della had decoded the final message of the dream. Its revelation of the source of her inner anxiety opened the door to her counseling needs. She needed help to become more independent. Also, she needed help to resolve issues related to her father's death and resulting anger against God. And definitely, she needed help in resolving her unhealthy relationship with her mother. These issues took months of counseling to resolve. Eventually, she became an emotionally healthy, independent woman equipped to enjoy life.

Chapter Nine

-DREAMS-
EXPRESSING FEARS

The emotion of fear is both destructive and beneficial. Without fear, we would engage in activities that could harm us. Fear imposes limits on our conduct and activities, thus saving us from situations and choices that would be destructive. However, excessive or irrational fear can paralyze us. Because of its volatile nature, every individual experiences episodes of fear. Whether consciously or unconsciously, fear permeates throughout our persona. Because of this fact, dreams frequently portray the emotion of fear.

The most terrifying emotion manifested through dreams is fear. It is expressed in the form of nightmares which awaken the sleeper in a state of panic. Even though the depicted scene is familiar, frequently the awakened sleeper is unaware of the source of the expressed fear. Being unable to eradicate the source of the fear, the dreamer continues to experience the emotional trauma over and over again. In order to remove the subconscious fear erupting with regularity in the victim's mind, the dreamer needs counseling help to uncover the subliminal terror. Dream analysis can be the prescription that brings peace to the troubled mind.

Hi, Doc! Can I talk to you a minute?"

The speaker was a young man, tastefully dressed, with a fine physique. I had seen him around the church a few times and been informed that he was the husband of one of our young ladies.

"I'm not sure I know your name," I responded.

"Randolph," he replied. "Dan Randolph."

"What can I do to help you, Dan?" I volunteered.

"Well, I am graduating in June from the University of Chicago," he responded.

"That's wonderful!" I commented. "Congratulations on completing your degree."

"Well, there is a little problem," he countered. "You see, in order to graduate, I have to go to the office of the university and pick up my diploma."

"What is the problem with that?" I inquired.

With a sheepish look on his face, Dan replied, "The University Office is on the fourteenth floor of the administration building and I am afraid to go up in the elevator. They won't send me my diploma, so I have a problem."

Hearing his dilemma, I asked an additional question: "Is riding an elevator the only area in which you have fear?"

"Oh no!" he admitted with a grin. "I have fear of just about everything. My wife, Sue, and I were married last summer. As an airline stewardess, she had free tickets to go to Hawaii for our honeymoon. I went on the plane, but only after I was half-drunk. I fear flying with a passion. I even dream about it," he acknowledged.

"Tell me your dream," I requested.

"Oh, I dream I am getting on a plane," Dan replied. "But before the plane can take off, I wake up in a panic state. This is a recurring dream, one I have had a number of times."

"Your dream is understandable," I commented. "It is the story of your life at the present time."

"What do you mean?" Dan asked. "How is it the story of my life?"

"Let me explain my statement," I added. "A moving vehicle such as a train, plane, or car is symbolic of a person moving through life. Your getting on a plane symbolizes your forward movement through life. Before the plane takes off, figuratively speaking, before you can move forward with your life plans, you wake up in a panic. Isn't that the story of your life at the present time?"

"Yes," Dan admitted. "That is my situation in life at the present time. Fear has paralyzed me to the point that I cannot live the life I desire."

Dan proceeded to tell me of other fears he had. He was afraid to drive under overpasses on the expressway; he was afraid to leave the city limits because it was too far from medical attention if he needed it; he had panic attacks thinking about having a heart attack. On and on he went describing his fear-wracked life.

Listening to the description of his life, my initial diagnosis of Dan's case led me to believe he was suffering from agoraphobia. This is a fear that comes from within, producing panic, weakness, and palpitations. When these nervous feelings arise, the sufferers experience a repeated assault. In addition to the original fear, sufferers experience the added fear of not obtaining help quickly enough and thus making a spectacle of themselves in front of others.

"You seem to have a very deep-seated problem," I concluded. "I believe you are beyond my expertise. I suggest you seek professional counseling elsewhere."

"I've been to two counselors," Dan replied. "They gave me some pills which didn't help. My wife told me you did counseling so I thought I would talk to you."

We discussed his problem further. In light of his limited financial resources and his school schedule, I agreed to begin counseling with him. At our first session, I informed him the first step to overcoming his fear was to understand its source. "In your case," I counseled, "your fear is coming from within, not from some outside stimulus. To understand this type of fear, we need to examine fearful experiences in your background, which have conditioned you to feel unwarranted panic."

With that request, Dan began to relate terrifying experiences he had as a child. He told how as a four-year-old, he was accustomed to leaning out of the second-story apartment window, watching for his father to come home from work. One day, as he performed this ritual, he leaned out too far, entangling his clothes in a flagpole holder. After squirming around for a moment, he found himself dangling from the flagpole high above the street. Eventually, his screaming brought his mother to his rescue but not before his fear was indelibly recorded on his mind.

Another fearful experience of childhood remained vivid in his mind. When he was five, his parents took him for a walk down a street in Chicago. They stopped at a tavern for a drink and instructed Dan to sit on the tavern step and wait for them. Becoming bored with waiting, Dan wandered down the street looking at objects in store windows. When he decided to return to the tavern steps, he couldn't find his way back. Terrified at being lost, he ran in panic up and down streets seeking his parents. Eventually, a policeman stopped him. When Dan could not tell the policeman where he was supposed to be, he was taken to the police station to await his neglectful parents. After a period of time, his parents were reunited with him at the police station. Being lost and separated from loved ones left a deep emotional scar on his psyche.

Dan also had a frightening experience in an elevator. Traveling on vacation, the family stopped in a strange town and rented a room in a hotel. Dan, a ten-year-old, was sent from the eighth floor to the lobby to get a paper. As he rode the elevator down, it became stuck between floors. His screaming alerted the hotel staff to his plight but it was an hour before he was rescued from his confinement in the elevator.

On and on, Dan related one story after another regarding terrifying childhood experience. Hearing his account of traumatic childhood experiences, I could understand why his mind was conditioned to subconscious fear. For a number of weeks, we discussed openly these traumatic experiences and how they had impacted his mind with latent emotional feelings erupting spontaneously in his mind at the slightest stimulus. Once stimulated, Dan experienced panic spasms, which included missed heartbeats, tightness across the chest, inability to take a deep breath, headaches, and, if away from home, an overwhelming desire to escape to surroundings where he knew he could calm down and the panic would abate. These symptoms originated from his sensitized mental responses to fear.

Once we had analyzed extensively the source of his irrational fears, we moved to the second step in overcoming agoraphobia. This involved learning to cope with the symptoms. I began this portion of his treatment by asking: "How do you react when one of these symptoms manifests itself?"

"I go berserk!" he exclaimed. "Many times, I have had my wife drive me to the emergency room because I thought I was having a heart attack."

"It appears," I counseled, "you have to learn to float."

Dan looked at me with a quizzical grin and replied: "You are not talking about swimming, I am sure."

"No," I replied, "but the principle is the same. When panic begins to grip you, you must play a mind game with yourself. Say to yourself: Here comes the river of my panic. I am going to float across this turbulent water until I reach the safety of the other side. Then just imagine yourself floating across the abyss. Don't fight it! Relax and patiently wait until the panic subsides. If you can learn to float, you can begin to overcome your anxiety. Do you think you can do that?"

"I can try," Dan replied.

Dan returned for his next appointment with minor success to report. On one occasion the previous week, he had averted a panic attack by floating. As the weeks progressed, he found more successes for his effort. I kept reassuring him that patience and a correct attitude toward panic would eventually bring him frequent success. Emphatically, I stressed, the key to failure or success lies in attitude...relax, float, be patient.

After a few weeks of partial success coping with his panic, Dan reported he had experienced another dream. I requested he share it with me.

"Is there such a thing as a dream series?" he asked.

"Certainly," I replied. "Some people have the same dream with a further episode each time."

"Well, that is my experience," Dan asserted. "Remember I told you about my getting on the plane and then waking up before we took off. Well in my dream this time, I boarded the plane and took my seat. Immediately, the plane left the runway and we were airborne. At that point, I awakened. What do you make of that?" he asked.

I responded by saying: "I will say the same thing I said regarding your earlier dream. This dream also is the story of your life. In the first dream, you awaken before the plane takes off. We interpreted that to mean your life was going nowhere because of your paralyzing fear. Now with counseling, you have gained some knowledge of your sensitized emotions and why you have these panic attacks. With this knowledge, you are making progress overcoming your fear. The symbolism of boarding the plane and taking off signifies your progress. Naturally, you awaken before you arrive at your destination because you still have not overcome your problem. But you are making progress. Does that interpretation of your dream make sense?" I asked.

"Yes, I am beginning to get the picture," Dan replied. "I have a long way to go but I am experiencing some success in coping with my attacks. Someday, I hope I will be able to handle all my episodes of panic."

The process of recovery was long. Although Dan was able to function on a limited scale, it took a few years to experience stress-free living. Agoraphobia is similar to alcoholism. One never completely overcomes it; one only learns to cope with it. A relapse can occur at any time if sufficient stress is allowed to build up.

I suggested one additional factor of the healing process to Dan. It was that he seek a strong relationship with God. The basis for my suggestion was that all fear in the last analysis is the fear of death. To overcome the fear of death, a person needs the assurance of everlasting life found in Jesus Christ. Dan was open to my counsel and joined a theological study group that I taught. After proper instruction, he professed his faith and began to walk with the Lord on a daily basis. Faith, that he is a child of God and that nothing could separate him from the love of God has been the crowning achievement in overcoming Dan's inner fears. Today, years later, he is a successful executive and a committed Christian.

****

Julia was a single mother of a nine-month-old girl named Tammy. Julia's live-in boyfriend, John, the father of the child, shared the home with her. He was a kind, considerate man who provided much help in parenting. John would arise at night to change Tammy's diaper or rock her to sleep. In spite of the wholesome environment prevailing in the home, Julia was plagued by a recurring, terrifying dream.

In a recent episode of this dream, Julia related, she saw John and Tammy in a bathtub full of water. Tammy was seated on John's lap enjoying her bath. As she watched the two playing in the bathwater, she saw Tammy slip forward down past John's leg and her head disappeared beneath the water. John was unaware of the infant's dilemma for a couple of minutes. Observing this, Julia raced forward and pulled her daughter from under the water. The infant was unconscious and Julia was trying desperately to revive her daughter when she awakened in a state of panic.

After listening to Julia relate her dream, I commented that it had to be terrifying to experience that type of a scene over and over again.

"You are right!" she lamented. "I am not sure I can stand it much longer. I am missing out on sleep. It is making me so nervous I don't eat right and I am just a mess."

"Have you seen a medical doctor?" I inquired.

"Oh yes," she replied, "but he just gave me the runaround. He said it is my nerves. He offered to give me a tranquilizer prescription but I didn't feel that was the solution to my problem, so I refused it. Recently, my boss noticed me crying a lot at work. When I told him my symptoms, he suggested I needed psychological help, so here I am."

"He's right," I commented. "Fear that is expressing itself so vividly will not be removed by taking tranquilizers. They might temporarily grant relief by relaxing you, but the problem will still be there. What you need," I added, "is to discover the source of your fear and exonerate it from your mind."

"That sounds great but how can it be done?" Julia asked.

"That is where counseling comes in," I replied. "You and I, together, need to look at your past experiences to determine what are the roots of your present fear, a fear bubbling up from your subconscious and giving you horrible nightmares." Your nightmares," I continued, "are expressing great fear, which is within you. Because the setting of these dreams is in your home and involves your child, this symbolizes that you are being threatened by someone or some situation very close to you. In light of that fact, I must begin our search for the basis of your fear by examining your home situation. Let me ask you a direct question. Do you have any fear that your live-in boyfriend might harm your little girl? I ask this question because in your dream, John is the one who accidentally allows her to slip under the water."

"Oh, no!" she exclaimed. "I have complete confidence in John. I know he loves Tammy and would never harm her."

"If the dream is not expressing actual fear regarding your daughter, then we have to look for another basis for the fear," I commented. "It appears your mind is using your daughter as a substitute for someone else. To uncover the hidden source of your fear, let us move further back in your life. Tell me about frightening experiences you have had."

In answer to my question, Julia began an overview of her life. Her father was an alcoholic and her parents divorced when she was six. Three years later, her mother married a divorced man who had a son four years older than Julia. When Julia was twelve, her stepbrother raped her. Her mother did not believe her story, so Julia had to fight her own battle with her stepbrother. Later when she was a teenager, Julia had many conflicts with her stepfather. He yelled at her a lot and on occasion would slap her. Again, her mother would not take Julia's part in these arguments. The result was that Julia developed deep anger against her mother, resulting in emotional separation. Julia left home as soon as she graduated from high school.

Hearing Julia describe her dysfunctional family, I asked a pertinent question: "Who constitutes your family today?" I inquired.

"I have no close family now," Julia answered. "I have forgiven my stepbrother for his action but I don't want him around me. I seldom see my mother or talk to her. Surprisingly, now that I am out of the home, I have a better relationship with my stepfather than with any of the other family members. He and I can have a civil conversation but not often."

"You must have someone," I remarked, "whom you are close to. Someone who can be considered family."

"Yes, I do," Julia replied. "I have two cousins who have always been there for me if I needed to talk with someone. I would go to them for advice and comfort."

"Are you still in close contact with them?" I asked. As I raised that question, tears formed in Julia's eyes. I could see our conversation had touched a sensitive nerve. Waiting a moment for her to gain her composure, I continued to pursue my inquiry by asking. "What is your relationship with your cousins now?"

Julia avoided the question. "They are the only family I have," she sobbed. "I could always count on them to be there when I needed them. When I left home, my oldest cousin took me in. She was a mother figure to me because my own mother showed no interest in me."

Pausing to catch her breath, I waited for Julia to tell me the rest of the story. When she hesitated, I asked again: "And what is your relationship with your cousin now?"

"That is the problem," she commented with a quivering voice. "I feel my cousin has rejected me. Since she married, she doesn't come around to see me and she won't even return my phone calls. She is acting just like my mother did towards me."

"And that brings up a lot of bad memories that scare you, I suspect."

"It certainly does," Julia replied. "I had thought she would always be there for me but she isn't."

Nodding my head, I commented: "That explains the dream."

"How can you say that?" Julia asked.

"The dream," I asserted, "was expressing fear of losing someone close to you. True, in the dream, it was your daughter, Tammy, you feared losing. Yet you admitted you had no actual fear of Tammy being hurt by John. In that case, the fear being expressed in the dream has to be a substitution of someone else being lost to you. Sometimes the mind substitutes another person for the actual person because it is too painful for the dreamer to admit the truth. Your fear of losing Tammy is similar to your fear of losing your cousin's love and acceptance."

We talked at length regarding her fear of losing contact with her older cousin. In order to verify this was the source of her fear, I asked when the nightmares began. Julia acknowledged they started soon after she had lost contact with her cousin. She had called and received no answer. Then she drove over to her cousin's apartment and knocked on the door. Even though she was sure her cousin was home, the cousin did not answer the door. All this discussion was mingled with Julia's tears.

The next counseling session added additional insight to the basis of Julia's fear. She reported she had experienced another disturbing dream, similar to the one she had described to me earlier. In this dream, it was not John but her younger cousin, Ann, who was in the bathtub with Tammy. In this pantomime, Ann allowed Tammy to slip under the water, resulting in Julia's panic-stricken awakening.

"What is your relationship with this cousin?" I inquired.

"The same as with my other cousin," Julia replied. "I fear I have lost her friendship also. She has not replied to any of my recent inquires. I can't believe both of them would cut me off that way."

Summing up what Julia had just said, I remarked: "Your mind is getting honest in revealing truth. Notice in this dream, it is your cousin, Ann, who endangers Tammy. That symbolism is saying you are angry at Ann." Following the interpretation of her dream, I added: "I imagine your cousins' actions reminded you of how your mother treated you. To have to go through the emotional wringer of rejection again would be something to fear."

"It is," she asserted. "I can't imagine the same thing happening to me again."

"So you have been carrying this fear of rejection the last couple of months," I submitted. "It appears your subconscious fear has been manifested in your nightly horror movie."

We discussed at length the emotional implications of this fear. Once the subject had been thoroughly discussed, I proposed: "Understanding the source of your fear, I believe you should be relieved of those disturbing nightly pantomimes."

In the weeks that followed the revelation of her fear source, Julia experienced fewer and fewer episodes of terrifying nightmares. Within a few months, she regained nights of peaceful sleep.

****

Denny was an emerging pre-teenager, twelve years of age. He lived with his father, mother, and a younger sister. For a period of two months, Denny had been experienced frightening nightmares. All his dreams had their location in the family home, either downstairs in the family room or upstairs in the hallway leading to his parents' bedroom. In his dreams, Denny would see horrible-looking beasts lurking behind furniture or hiding around doors. The sight of these terrifying creatures caused him to awaken screaming with fear.

Denny's mother, Doris, called for an appointment and brought him to my office. I visited briefly with her, regarding background information relating to Denny. Particularly, I asked her if she knew of any frightening experiences her son had encountered. Doris informed me she knew of none, except the family viewing of the film, The Exorcist. "Denny," she acknowledged, "became very upset with some of the scenes in that film." She expressed regret regarding exposing the children to that movie. Otherwise, she knew of no terrifying experiences; but she knew Denny had a problem. Motherly love now propelled her to seek help for her terrified son.

Once I had gathered background information from Doris, I excused her and began a private conversation with Denny. My opening remark was the statement: "I understand you have been experiencing terrifying nightmares."

"Yes," replied Denny. "They are scary and they make me afraid."

"How afraid have they made you?" I asked.

"Afraid enough that I won't go down into the family room by myself or upstairs alone to my bedroom. I stay in the kitchen with mother most of the time."

"How long have you been experiencing these nightmares?" I inquired.

"Oh, about two months," Denny replied. "They started shortly after we all went to see the movie, The Exorcist."

"From what your mother told me, that movie really scared you," I remarked. "What part of the movie was scary?"

"It was the part where the demon was in the woman," Denny commented. "I wonder if the devil is in me because I do some bad things."

"Where would you get that idea?" I asked.

Denny responded: "Well, when I accidentally broke a lamp last week, Dad said, you must have the devil in you to be so bad."

"You don't really believe that, do you?" I questioned.

"I don't think so," Denny responded. "But I worry sometimes about it."

Knowing Denny was a twelve-year-old-boy, my approach to help him overcome internal fear regarding being filled with the devil had to be quite simple. Therefore, I determined to free his mind of worry by reassuring him from the standpoint of his faith.

"Do you believe in God and attend church?" I asked.

"Yes," Denny responded. "I go to church every Sunday and I partake of the sacrament."

"Then you should have no fear of being filled with the devil," I assured him. "Satan and God cannot both live in a person at the same time. If Jesus is in your heart, Satan cannot be there also."

Denny nodded his head in agreement as he thought on my statement. Then he responded by asking: "But why am I having these bad dreams?"

"I believe," I told him, "you have some strong anger against someone in your household. The fact that your dream settings are confined to your house would indicate to me that you have fear of someone close to you." Knowing the answer to my next question, I still asked it because I wanted Denny to concentrate on the individuals who constituted his family. "Who," I asked, "lives in your house with you?"

Denny listed them quickly: "My mother, father, and sister."

"Which of those are you angry at, Denny?" I inquired.

"I'm not mad at anyone in my family," he replied.

"You might believe that," I answered, "yet your dreams seem to be giving a different answer. Let's look at each person individually. Take your younger sister, for instance. You have no problems with her?" I inquired.

"Oh, no," he said. "We get along fine. She sometimes gets in my stuff but not very often."

"Then there is your mother," I commented. "I can't believe you have angry feelings regarding your mother. I remember you said you feel comfortable being around her."

"I love my mother," Denny replied. "She always tries to protect me when I get in trouble."

"That leaves your father. How do you feel about your father?" I asked.

Denny hesitated a moment before replying: "I love my dad."

"Does he always show love for you?" I asked.

"Well, sometimes he spanks me but I deserve it," Denny responded.

I could see it was going to be hard getting Denny to say anything negative about his dad. My suspicion was Denny did not know his true feelings regarding his father. Denial of one's true emotions is not uncommon, especially among children. This is because children do not understand it is possible to feel both love and hostility toward another person at the same time.

Therefore, I realized Denny was not readily going to admit he harbored hostility toward his father.

The next time Denny came for an appointment, I approached him with a new proposal designed to break through the barrier of singular feeling. "Let's play a game this week," I suggested. "I will give you two sentences I want you to complete. The first one is: I love my dad because... You complete the sentence and then I will give you the second one. It will be: I am angry at my dad because..." After I explained how the game was to be played, we started.

"First sentence, Denny: I love my dad because... Complete it now."

Denny replied by affirming: "I love my dad because he takes us out for ice cream cones."

"Good!" I exclaimed. "Now complete the second sentence: I am angry at my Dad because..."

Denny hesitated a moment and then replied: "I am angry at my Dad because he yells at me a lot."

"A good answer," I replied. "Now let's do the same cycle again."

Each time we played the game, Denny would speak of something he liked about his dad. But, also, each time he would delve deeper into his hostile feelings. Before long, he was expressing his feelings about getting slapped about, kicked when he was slow to follow orders, and finally he spoke of the strappings his father gave him with a belt. Slowly but steadily, the game uncovered through verbal speech the feelings Denny had been holding deep inside.

In light of the information I gleaned regarding the father's disciplinary treatment of his son, I requested the father come for consultation. I explained to the father the damaging consequences resulting from his approach to discipline. The father was shocked that his method of discipline, derived from his Eastern European heritage, would be detrimental to his son.

After further discussion, he agreed to modify his conduct and begin to show more love toward Denny.

The results of Denny's open verbalization of hostile feelings and the father's change in relating to his son were soon evident in Denny's life. The nightmares tapered off and harmony began to be experienced in the family household. We continued counseling for a couple of months, expanding on our understanding of the family problems. Six months later, during the summer season, Denny spent a week camping in the woods with his scout troop. His terrifying beasts were an item of the past.

Chapter Ten

-DREAMS-
GOD'S SECOND
LANGUAGE

In the Christian tradition, dreams have been God's second language. Within the pages of Holy Scripture, time and again, God has revealed His message to mortals through the medium of a dream. Beginning with Jacob's dream of a ladder extending to heaven, God spoke identifying Himself to Jacob as the God of his grandfather, Abraham, and his father, Isaac. After identifying Himself, God promised a blessing upon Jacob and his descendants (Genesis 28:10-17). Later, God spoke through a dream to Pharaoh which was interpreted by Joseph. This dream told of seven years of plenty and seven years of famine, which were coming upon the land of Egypt (Genesis 41:1-8). About eighteen centuries later, God's voice was heard by another man, named Joseph, through a dream. God instructed this Joseph "to take Mary as your wife, for the child conceived in her is from the Holy Spirit. She will bear a son, and you are to name him Jesus" (Matthew 1:20-21). Forty years later, Simon Peter had a dream while sleeping on a rooftop in Joppa. As a blanket was lowered before him containing animals, he was told to rise, kill, and eat. Peter's quandary regarding the order to eat forbidden animals led him to interpret the dream as meaning the Gospel of salvation was for all people, not just the Jews (Acts 10:9-16).

God's use of His second language is not limited to Biblical times. He still speaks to individuals in our present era. If that is true, you might ask, why aren't more people aware of this fact? An excellent answer to that question was given by George Bernard Shaw in his play, Saint Joan. In that play, Shaw has the Maid of Orleans, Joan of Arc, reply to the question of King Charles. "Why don't the voices come to me? I am king, not you," Charles asked. To his question, Joan replies: "They do come to you, but you do not hear them. You have not sat in the field in the evening listening to the thrilling of the bells in the air after they stopped ringing. When the angelus rings you cross yourself and have done with it, but if you prayed from your heart, and listened to the thrilling of the bells in the air after they stopped ringing, you would hear the voices as well as I do" (Saint Joan, Scene V).

To paraphrase George Bernard Shaw's answer, prayer and meditation are the human qualities necessary for hearing the voice of God. Yes, God resorts to His second language with those who meditate upon Him.

Through the years, I have used the Divine message found in individuals' dreams to help the dreamers understand themselves. For this chapter, however, I have chosen not to report on dream analysis per se but to relate dreams which personal friends have experienced wherein they heard the voice of God. I do not profess to understand the occurrence of their experiences, but I cannot deny their reality. I report these dream experiences as evidence God still speaks through His second language.

- -

Nola was sixteen and a junior in high school. She lived with her parents and older brother. These were working class people manifesting the traditional American qualities of honest labor, integrity, and thrift. One particular identity, that of Bible-believing members of a Wesleyan Methodist Church, exemplified the family unit.

Nola, the youngest child, had scarlet fever during early childhood. This illness left her with serious heart problems. Her condition restricted normal physical activity forcing her to become a semi-invalid. Throughout the afflicted years of her childhood, Nola's family and church congregation prayed for her healing. Year after year, they continued praying while her physical condition grew steadily worse. By the middle of her junior year of high school, the weakness of her heart restricted her to a bed, located upstairs in the family home.

After a month of confinement to her bed, Nola experienced a marvelous dream one night. Jesus appeared to her and said, "I have heard the prayers spoken in your behalf. You are healed!" With that startling pronouncement, Jesus' presence faded away and Nola awoke.

Nola lay in the darkness thinking about the statement of her Lord. Then, acting on faith, she threw back her bedcovers and swung her feet out onto the floor. Although she had not been on her feet for weeks except for bathroom needs, she stood up, turned on the light and walked about the room. After walking around excitedly a few minutes, she climbed back into bed and finally went back to sleep.

In the morning, Nola arose from her bed and dressed herself. Then she proceeded to walk down the stairs to the kitchen where her mother was preparing breakfast. Seeing her daughter walk into the kitchen shocked her mother greatly. Screaming, the mother shouted: "What are you doing up? You should be in bed!" Nola calmed her mother by replying: "It's OK. I have been healed." After the astonishing announcement had been absorbed by the mother and they were seated at the kitchen table, Nola related the dream and what the Lord had said to her.

In spite of their strong faith, Nola's parents had lingering doubts concerning their daughter's healing. As soon as possible, they took Nola to their family doctor for a checkup. After careful examination, the doctor could find no evidence of the earlier heart problem. Nola was declared completely cured by her doctor. God's message to Nola, spoken through a dream, was now substantiated by medical science.

Nola returned to school and completed her secondary education. Following graduation, she volunteered to teach music at an Indian mission school in South Dakota. There she has enjoyed normal health and has served a number of years as a missionary.

****

J.B. retired from farming in 1950. He and his wife, Grace, moved from their farm to a nearby small community where he purchased an acre of land at the edge of town. His love of farming prompted him to keep one cow for their personal milk supply.

A few years after retirement, J.B. suffered a mild heart attack. His doctor restricted his activity, thereby forcing his wife to perform the twice-daily task of milking the cow. One particular winter day, as the shadows of darkness were falling over the land, J.B. was reclining on a sofa in his front room. He was alone in the house because Grace had gone to the barn to milk the cow. In semi-darkness, he dozed on the sofa. Suddenly a bright light filled the room and Jesus appeared, standing before him. The Lord spoke to him, saying: "Come along, J.B., it is time to go." Without any emotion or fear, J.B. replied: "I am willing to go, Lord, but Grace is going to be terribly shocked to come in from the barn and find me dead." The Lord steadfastly continued to look lovingly at him for a brief moment. Then the brightness began to fade and the apparition of the Lord disappeared. Once semi-darkness returned to the room, J.B. shook himself awake and sat up. Looking around the room, he observed all was normal.

The next day, when I made a pastoral call, J. B. related his dream to me. After hearing it, I asked him what message he thought the dream was conveying. J.B. replied: "I believe the Lord has granted me a little more time. When death does come to me someday, I will not be afraid."

Five years later, J.B. died in his sleep. The Lord had come for him a second time, and this time J.B. went home with Him. At the funeral service, I related in my eulogy his conversation with the Lord that occurred on the earlier occasion. It brought comfort to all who mourned his passing.

****

John grew to adulthood with a great reverence for God. This reverence had its foundation through experiencing the reality of God in daily family worship in the home. During the teen years, certain morally wrong conduct resulted in his developing an overshadowing fear of the Almighty. Knowing God was a holy Being, John was afraid that one day the Lord would appear before him in judgment. That thought filled John with internal emotional panic.

When John was eighteen, God spoke to him. The voice was audible to John's heart, as real as if another human being had spoken. Distinctly, John heard the words: "You are going to be a minister." Responding to this command, John gave his life in obedience to this Divine calling to the Gospel ministry.

Throughout his college and seminary years, the fear of a personal confrontation with God did not diminish. In his first parish, John felt tense whenever he walked into his empty church. When walking past the open door of the sanctuary, John always avoided looking at the altar because he feared seeing the living God.

In the second year of his ministry, John experienced an illuminating dream. In his dream, John was dusting the pews in the church sanctuary. This symbolism undoubtedly originated from his memory experience as a part-time church custodian during college days. While he was at work, suddenly the sanctuary was filled with a brilliant light. Without raising his eyes, John knew the Lord had appeared to him. Terrifying panic seized his heart, freezing him in motion. Then, just as suddenly as fear had swept over him, it was replaced with blissful peace and joy. While he continued to experience this radiant feeling of peace, the brilliant light filling the sanctuary began to fade away. After a moment, it was gone. At that point, John lifted his eyes and looked around. Everything appeared normal within the sanctuary. With that observation, the dream ended and he awoke.

John interpreted the dream as a message from God. The message was that an individual should not fear the presence of the Almighty. Instead of bringing wrathful judgment, God's presence brings peace and joy. From that time onward, John was freed from fear of meeting God. Encountering God was now a glorious expectation.

CONCLUSION

The preceding counseling cases involving dream analysis have been written to inform you regarding the significance of dreams to understanding self. It is hoped that this material will motivate you to seek personal insights from your dreams. Using techniques and knowledge gleaned from these case studies, you should be able to analyze many of your personal dreams. Remember, all dreams are a private letter to oneself. They are a pantomime revealing personal inner conflicts. We dream when unresolved problems from waking life press upon us during sleep. Our subconscious mind struggles with these unresolved problems and seeks to solve them. We may not always appreciate the truth revealed, but that truth can be beneficial to us. Inner truth regarding self can set us free from psychological problems.

I challenge you to examine your dreams and to be honest in accepting their revelations. They will not lead you astray. Accept them as a part of God's blessing of guidance to you. Illuminated by your dreams, you can find the doorway to emotional health. Walk through it to a more abundant life.

Do you wish to help friends find a happier life through interpretation of their personal dreams? Then send them an autographed copy of this book designated as a gift from you for their birthday, anniversary, Christmas present, etc. A copy will be sent in your name by sending $15.00 plus $2.00 for postage to: Lloyd E. Shaw, Box 371, Collinsville, IL 62234. Allow three weeks for delivery.

Printed in the United States
23349LVS00004B/496

9 781418 400590